VEGANIC GARDENING

Describes fully an alternative system of horticulture which avoids all chemical or animal fertilizers, is more productive and less labour-intensive than conventional methods, and produces fruit and vegetables that are both tastier and healthier.

VEGANIC

GARDENING

The Alternative System for Healthier Crops

by

Kenneth Dalziel O'Brien

THORSONS PUBLISHING GROUP

First published 1986

© KENNETH DALZIEL O'BRIEN 1986

British Library Cataloguing in Publication Data

O'Brien, Kenneth Dalziel
Veganic gardening:
the alternative system for healthier crops
1. Gardening
I. Title
635'   SB450.97

ISBN 0-7225-1208-2

Published by Thorsons Publishers Limited, Wellingborough, Northamptonshire, NN8 2RQ, England

Printed in Great Britain by
Hazell Watson & Viney Limited
Member of BPCC plc
Aylesbury, Bucks, England

3 5 7 9 10 8 6 4 2

CONTENTS

		Page
	Introduction	7
1.	What is Veganic Gardening?	9
2.	The Structure of the Soil	13
3.	Clearing the Ground	15
4.	Permanent Raised Garden Beds	18
5.	Veganic Compost Making, Seed Sowing and Planting	23
6.	A New Approach to Weeds	33
7.	Watering	35
8.	Outdoor Salad Crops	37
9.	Vegetables	45
10.	Herbs	61
11.	Growing Fruit	70
12.	Growing under Glass	85
13.	Garden Design	101
14.	Basic Tools and Equipment	130
	Glossary	132
	Appendix 1 Assembling a Cold Frame	134
	Appendix 2 Dimensions of a Twin Compost Bin	137
	Suppliers	139
	Useful Addresses	141
	Index	143

INTRODUCTION

This book is for all gardeners, or would-be gardeners, of any age, who like to do things for themselves.

It contains new ways of cultivating the soil which will inspire fresh interest in 'old hands', as well as simple step-by-step directions to help the beginner.

No previous knowledge will be required to grow clean, healthy, and tasty salads, culinary vegetables, fruit and herbs, and at far less cost than would have been possible by any other method.

Raised beds of uncompacted soil make it possible to sow seed or plant seedlings and vegetable plants at the earliest dates, although soil, like everything else, needs care and attention, not only for our own benefit, but for the well-being of future generations.

No one at present is in a position to say what the soil of his own country is capable of producing when the orthodox destructive customs prevalent today give way to surface cultivation, and the only form of manure applied to the soil is a herbally activated vegetable compost, spread on and amalgamated into the surface soil.

In the garden as a whole, the beauty of a single specimen tree or flowering shrub will grace a lawn, lending enchantment to the view from the house, while beyond it may be a 'surprise' corner with its neat rows of vegetables and fruit blending in with the overall garden theme, but perhaps concealed from view by cordon or espalier apples.

By co-ordinating the garden in all its aspects with the life of the family in the home, a happy relationship of mutual aid and enjoyment may be established. This book aims to show how this can be accomplished with the minimum of effort. With its help, even the beginner should be capable of producing top-quality salads, culinary vegetables, herbs and fruit of fine flavour, as well as planning out the garden, selecting decorative trees, shrubs and foliage plants for year-round appeal.

Veganic culture is gentle in every way and the following chapters will, it is hoped, enable you to achieve not only a productive garden, but one of absorbing interest and enduring pleasure.

CHAPTER 1

WHAT IS VEGANIC GARDENING?

The horticultural system set forth in this book relies on materials entirely from the vegetable kingdom — with or without natural minerals. The term *veganic* (from *v*egetable and or*ganic*) was first used by Geoffrey L. Rudd. It denotes a clear distinction between conventional chemical-based systems and organic ones based on animal manures.

The system is that pioneered and developed by the author's family over more than four decades of amateur, commercial and professional practice. It combines not only the use of purely vegetable compost, but also the following features:

1. no digging, i.e. surface cultivation only;
2. non-compaction of the soil;
3. a special, and perhaps unique, approach to weed control.

Although the Dalziel O'Brien family pioneered the new system, credit must go to Maye Bruce for introducing the method of composting that is a cornerstone of the system. Her book *From Vegetable Waste to Fertile Soil* (1938) greatly influenced us, and it led us to make our first such compost in the garden of our house in 1940.

In those days an average heap took five to six weeks to mature during the summer period, but now, with a larger bin 4 feet (1.2 m) square and 3½ feet (1.7 m) high and using only very fine soft materials, summer heaps are ready

to use only two to three weeks after completion.

To advance from small-scale gardening using this type of compost to a much larger area of land for commercial cropping was quite another story. Nevertheless, we managed not only to make sufficient compost for large-scale commercial crop production but also to evolve a method of soil cultivation that resulted in better crops, yielding more palatable fruit and vegetables.

Part of the commercial holding just mentioned had been allocated to salad crops, so the early weed growth was used in full for compost making. After a while the weeds became less in number and more reliance was put on feeding the crops with a solution of compost in water, which compensated for the loss of bulk compost. The pioneering efforts, and their results over nine years, are described by Rosa Dalziel O'Brien in her book *Intensive Gardening* (Faber, 1956).

At present the system remains a purely manual one, and small-scale gardening is, and should forever remain, an enjoyable and beneficial human activity. Everyone with a garden or allotment can benefit by growing vegetables, herbs, fruit and flowers and in the case of gardens, ornamental trees, shrubs and ground cover in a cleaner soil without recourse to the use of animal wastes which, even when composted, continue to carry the spores of disease harmful to both plant and man. It is generally acknowledged that the spores of clubroot, a disease of the cabbage family, are spread in animal dung, and the salmonella bacillus, which can cause an acute form of food poisoning in humans, can occur in animal wastes. Without wishing to labour the point unduly, one may also ask what happens to the excreta of animals infected with such highly infectious and serious diseases as anthrax, brucellosis and husk. It is such a well-known fact that horse dung carries tetanus as to be scarcely worth mentioning!

In addition there is now an ever-increasing anxiety that various 'medicines' and growth-promoting chemical substances added to the feed of the farm animals reared only for slaughter at a few months old are finding their way into human beings with an allotted span of three score years and ten. Those that are not may well be spread in dung on intensive organic holdings, to be taken up by the roots of the growing salad, vegetable and cereal crops and hence eventually ingested by humans. Soil, flora and fauna, on which all life on this planet eventually depends, are affected. It cannot be truly maintained that our vegetables, fruits, cereals and nuts are better for our health when grown with animal organics: we are in fact absorbing pollutants as dangerous as those which in other ways we are trying to avoid.

Yet the fouling of land where crops are being grown for people to eat goes on, as many vegetable growers still believe that animal organics are the only source of lasting fertility. But is this really true? Consider the unturned soil of the forest floor. Here all forms of life function at their respective levels. This is an organization of efficiency that is as near perfection as one may find.

Advocates of animal organics recog-

nize that adding chemical fertilizers which stimulate the growth of plants does little to sustain or increase the teeming millions of soil organisms and earthworms. Rather, it creates an imbalance which renders them less efficient.

What these same people fail to appreciate, however, is that exactly the same basic error is made by adding animal organics. This not only introduces harmful types of bacteria and micro-organisms into the soil, in proportions far outside any found in nature; it also stimulates the quite unnatural growth in numbers of naturally occurring soil organisms which are needed to assimilate the foreign substances into the soil.

In short, animal organics, like chemical fertilizers, create a soil imbalance. For while the domestic animals' ancestors lived in an environment where, overall, a naturally balanced soil was maintained despite their presence, any isolated local imbalances would have been adjusted when the animals instinctively moved on so as not to destroy their source of food, giving the worms, insects and microscopic soil workers time to do their work of rendering the animal wastes as harmless as possible. In this way herbage and soil were kept in a reasonably healthy state.

A hint of the way in which the application of animal organics unbalances the soil is seen when cow dung is dropped on a pasture. Immediately, there is a stimulation of herbage growth. But a season later the coarser, less verdant plants are thriving while the finer grasses are set back or even destroyed. Where cattle are contained in fields and forced to graze the same area over and over again, not only are they absorbing their own wastes via the grasses, thus contributing to disease; they are also progressively depleting the fertility of the soil upon which the grazing plants depend, so that the pasture has continually to be 'rested' in order not just for the plants to grow, but for the stability of the soil upon which that growth depends to be restored.

To sum up, the animal matter in animal organics is a pollutant, which is a carrier of disease and even death. We need also to consider the ways soils are cultivated. Everywhere in the industrialized world today, large-scale cultivation is carried out by heavy machinery which through compaction causes serious damage to the soil's structure. Tractor wheels or caterpillar tracks exert considerable pressure not only downwards but sideways in the soil. This has a lasting and detrimental effect on the soil's capacity to sustain life. Even human feet can exert a considerable pressure on the soil's surface. Digging gardeners claim that their annual (or more frequent) exertions loosen up the soil after all the trampling during the growing season. So they dig the soil, not always without injury to themselves and then once more trample all over it! Compaction destroys soil life and hence fertility, and it is today increasingly recognized as a serious problem, which not only agricultural engineers but also all users of the land must do their best to minimize.

Under the veganic system, *complete* freedom from compaction of all sowing areas is achieved by dividing the land into permanent garden beds for the growing vegetables and soft fruits with paths between the beds. All work of cultivation, weeding, sowing and planting, etc., is done from the paths without treading on the soil of the beds. This practice brings with it the advantage that many of these operations are possible when the wetness of the soil after rain would make it impossible otherwise to work in the garden.

Covering the paths with clean new straw makes it possible to walk along them at any time of the year without getting muddy shoes.

A bed width of 4½ feet (1.37 m) and a path width of 15 inches (38 cm) have been found to be most suitable. (It is worth noting here that although the paths are permanently 'lost' to cultivation, this is more than compensated for by the closer spacing of the crop rows which the bed system allows.) In order for the soil to improve, it is essential that it is stabilized and that the top soil is kept at the top and not dug or ploughed under. The continual burying of the top soil is damaging to soil bacteria and other organisms, especially earthworms, which all have their own particular levels at which to operate.

Ploughing or digging means that the top 8 inches (20 cm) or so of soil – where most of the soil's vitality resides – becomes less efficient as an entity, as those organisms fortunate enough to survive the inversion have to recover their original positions before they can fully resume their functions. This again is most obvious in the case of earthworms.

In many cases, deep cultivation also keeps up the cycle of deep-rooted weeds – often the hardest to eradicate and the most vigorous growers – which rob the cultivated plants of food, light and water. The traditional methods of hoeing and harrowing or modern methods of destroying them with weed-killers will still not solve the problem of deep-rooted noxious weeds on ploughed or dug land.

On the other hand, were the soil to remain undisturbed for several years, soil life would return to normal, i.e. to that consistent with undisturbed soil; we would also find the deep-rooted weeds bring replaced by a finer type of plant, including long and short grasses.

Humus would be built up and the structure of the soil would improve. This sequence may be observed on any land left out of cultivation, but, and this is significant, once ploughing or digging begins again there is a return to the deep-rooted and creeping types of weeds.

The veganic system includes only shallow disturbance of the soil, without inversion. Only the top 3 to 4 inches (7.5 to 10 cm) are cultivated, and, as will be seen later, the scourge of the deep-rooted weed is eradicated.

Besides making more efficient use of the gardener's own energy (while offering considerably less cause for back pain!), this alternative system, which is more in harmony with nature, ensures that an ample supply of pure, rich humus is available, via the compost heap, for growing good-quality vegetables, herbs, fruit, nuts, flowers, trees and shrubs.

This safe and hygienic system is ideally suited to the home garden or allotment, and has proven successful on all types of soils.

CHAPTER 2

THE STRUCTURE OF THE SOIL

The soil is one of Nature's greatest marvels and any thoughtful and environmentally aware person will be concerned about how it is cultivated and generally cared for, whether in commercial cropping, on the allotment or in the home garden. This applies as much to fruit and flowers as to vegetables.

There are a number of soil types, each with its own structure and each capable of undergoing a lasting improvement in its fertility, workability and general condition. Soils are usually classified according to texture. This depends on the relative amounts of the different-sized mineral particles, sand, silt and clay, they contain. Texture is important because it affects the handling, aeration, drainage and nutrient content of the soil. Sand can be detected by its grittiness. Silt has a powder-like feel when dry. Clay feels smooth but the surface becomes polished when rubbed between the fingers and the soil is sticky when wet. A true loam is smooth and not gritty, silty or sticky when wet.

Sandy Soils

Sandy soils are generally the warmest and are very suitable for early vegetable crops; soft fruits can be grown successfully provided they are mulched and irrigated. Such soils are often described as being 'thirsty' or 'hungry', since their mineral particles, being relatively large, are without colloidal properties and retain little or no water between them. Sandy soils thus drain very quickly and during the summer can become dust-dry. So in order to grow good crops on a sandy soil there must be access to a water supply. At the same time a good supply of humus in the top few inches can act like a sponge and hold a lot of water. Very good specimens of conifers, azaleas, rhododendrons, brooms, heathers, some alpines and many bulbs can be grown. Although sandy soils are extremely easy to cultivate, they are nevertheless liable to 'blow away', and thus lose their stability.

Loam

Those fortunate enough to have a loam are indeed lucky, as it is the easiest soil to look after. A loam has a well-balanced proportion of sand, silt and clay particles, giving it an ideal texture, and is very productive. Aeration and drainage are good, and the soil insects and earthworms are very active, which makes for an excellent crumb structure.

Chalk and Limestone Soils

Often referred to as calcareous soils, these are naturally rich in lime (calcium carbonate) from the underlying bedrock. Many of these soils are only a few inches in depth and tend to lose any reserves of moisture during dry summer weather; it is essential to make sure that humus is added to the surface soil in the form of mulches. After heavy rain the soil tends to dry in hard, steely lumps, which are not easy to break down. If the clay content is at all high it normally takes a lot of skill to break it down using the traditional methods of tillage, such as digging and hoeing.

Clay Soils

At the other end of the scale are the clay soils, which are usually the most difficult to cultivate by traditional methods. This is due in the main to the fact that the particles are very small, and the spaces between them are, of course, tiny too. The result is that after rain the water is held in the tiny pore spaces, making the soil heavy and very difficult to work. As clay soils dry out, the minute particles stick together, so that a clay soil is like cement. It also expands when wet and shrinks when dry. So when it is wet, air cannot enter, and any root growth is much more restricted than on sandy soils.

Like sandy soils, clay soils benefit from the surface incorporation of vegetable compost; such humus helps to bind the particles together into crumbs; this in itself improves the drainage and assists in preventing water from lying on the soil's surface. However, clay soils are naturally rich in plant nutrients, although these are not always available since plant roots tend to follow cracks in the lower soil and fail to tap the nutrients in the surface soil lumps.

The Surface Soil and Subsoil

There is usually a marked difference between the humus and colour of the top layer of soil and the sub-soil, the top layer being darker. The top zone is important not only as a habitat for plants, but also for other living things like the soil insects, soil bacteria, and the largest of the soil's inhabitants – the earthworm. There are many species of earthworm, but only two of them make casts, which not only contain fine mineral matter but also tend to enrich the surface soil zone with plant foods. Earthworms are extremely beneficial to soils in other ways, notably by boring, perforating, loosening and thus creating pore spaces and rendering the soil pervious to rain.

The combined activities of all the soil inhabitants maintain a natural order, which is one of the factors in the improvement of all soils, whatever the type. To invert the topsoil by digging inevitably means displacing and burying the soil inhabitants in an unfamiliar, lower zone layer environment, away from the natural level in which they are actively engaged. After all, it is within the top 6 to 9 inches (15 cm to 23 cm) that seedlings and plant roots mostly develop.

Non-Compaction of Soils

In order for the surface soil to benefit from its inhabitants' assistance in the breakdown and assimilation of vegetable compost which has been applied, it is essential for this topsoil zone to remain not only at the top but also free of compaction, so that air and water can enter freely. In the regions of the world where winter brings snow and frost, any freezing and thawing, wetting and drying will have the effect of creating a crumb formation, providing again that the soil remains free of compaction, and this more open structure of the topsoil makes it a better place for plants to grow.

CHAPTER 3

CLEARING THE GROUND

It has been mentioned earlier that a bed and path method should be adopted in order to avoid compaction of the soil. The conversion to this method can be started at any time of the year, but preferably in early spring or early autumn. Measure and mark out the area, and clear away all plant debris and weeds using only a scrapper (see page 20) to assist in removal of the finer, softer type of weeds and a fork to lever out the coarser type of perennial ones. It is advisable to do this from an 8 by 1 inch (20 cm by 2.5 cm) board 5 or 6 feet (1.50 or 1.80 m) long which is supported at each end on a 2 by 2 inch (5 cm by 5 cm) bar of wood (see picture 1). Standing on the board ensures minimum compaction and compression of the soil. At all times keep the board on cleared soil, and not on growth to be cleared.

Start from a path and work inwards: after a short preparatory clearance, place the board on the two bars on the cleared area and then work always forward. Have a bucket or box nearby for putting in the annual soft weeds and another container for the coarser hard stems and roots. (It may also be convenient to have containers for stones, slugs, rubbish, etc., as in any garden.)

Clearing unwanted growth from the soil and assembling the compost heaps, fine and rough, are done simultaneously. Nothing is ever buried or left on the

Picture 1   Using a board supported by narrow bars to avoid compacting the soil.

soil surface as this only results in attracting slugs and pests. Be sure to exclude from any heap the materials listed as unsuitable in Chapter 5. The manner in which the fork is used has significance; when a deep root of thistle, dock or couch is encountered, insert the fork close to the root and merely lever till the root can be pulled out. Avoid turning the soil over in the usual 'fork-it-out' way. In other words endeavour to keep the topsoil where it really belongs – on the top.

It is interesting to note that when the soil is left undug and mulches of compost are applied to its surface, any odd pieces of old roots left in the ground automatically move nearer to the surface, so at the end of the season they can easily be removed.

Clearing Dense Weeds and Problem Soils

There may well be times when an actual allotment or garden plot has never been cultivated, or else has been left un-attended or only partially cultivated. Whatever the situation, and particularly with a plot composed of extremely heavy clay soil, it is more likely that an area will be overgrown with coarse perennial weeds and rank grasses. Tra-ditional methods of clearing such a plot entail a great deal of hard, laborious and even painful physical work. Any clear-ing involving rotovating the growth into the soil or the use of a flame gun, or even possibly using weedkiller to destroy the weed growth, will only result in creating more problems. Green material turned under will encourage slugs to proliferate and the soil bacteria to be thrown out of balance. A flame gun may burn off the surface growth but there will remain the roots of perennial weeds which will entail furth-er physical work. Weedkillers will eradi-cate only the top growth of weeds, will more than likely need repeated applica-tion, and will generally cause imbalance in the surface soil. These methods are costly and time-consuming. Digging or rotovating also damages the soil. The veganic method of clearing heavily infested land is to take advantage of a plant's tendencies to move its roots nearer to the soil's surface when it is deprived of light. To make use of this principle, aided by a decaying process of the top growth of weeds, etc., it is necessary to subject such growth to heat and moisture in order to speed up the decay, and this is done by applying lime, then a heavy straw cover and then

the herbal compost activator.

The use of this method ought, ideally, to be planned well in advance of any sowing and planting – certainly at least four weeks will need to be allowed. The following are required:

1. Sufficient new straw to cover an area to be cleared to a depth of 3 to 4 inches (7.5 cm to 10 cm). (Larger areas may be cleared section by section if necessary – the straw used on one section may be used on the next and possibly the next in turn.)
2. QR herbal activator solution, the same as used for the compost heap.
3. Garden lime.
4. Water.

First flatten the weed growth with either a wooden roller or else the back of a garden fork. Then spread a thin coating of lime followed by the cover-ing of straw. Water well by spraying and then sprinkle on the prepared herbal activator at the rate of one pint per 12 square yards (0.56 l per 10 sq.m). Finally spray again with water.

It is important to make sure the strawed area never dries out during the decaying period, which is usually be-tween three and four weeks. After the decaying period, rake off the surface straw and debris and either reserve for later use as straw layers in a rough compost heap or simply use again on the next section to be cleared.

Immediately afterwards, use the scrapper and fork to prepare the ground for the making of the garden beds in the usual manner, using the board sup-ported on the two bars as described above. Be sure to have a container for the debris.

It will be found that the roots of docks will be far easier to grip and pull out, levering with the fork, than it would have been thought possible, also the creeping types of weeds, such as couch and bindweed. Nevertheless, constant vigilance will be necessary in the first season or so, and any other young weeds must be removed as soon as they appear, to go on to the fine heap. After a few seasons of surface cultivation and applications of veganic compost, deep-rooted weeds will seldom be seen again. Digging the soil in the traditional manner and using animal organic wastes (dung, etc.) actually encourages the growth of coarse, persistent weeds, whereas the absence of such practices has the opposite effect – it discourages them.

Note that any weed growth that is to be left uncleared on any section must be cut, raked off and burnt, or composted if possible, to prevent the weeds spreading to any section already cleared.

CHAPTER 4

PERMANENT RAISED GARDEN BEDS

As already mentioned the basic requirement for the conversion of any vegetable and soft fruit growing area to the surface cultivation routine is to form the area into raised garden beds with paths in between. Such beds are an integral part of the veganic system and are essential for complete success.

The bed-and-path system confers a number of advantages. One is the ease with which any job, whether cultivating, weeding, sowing and planting, or collecting is managed from the paths. Another is the avoidance of treading or trampling on the soil in which the plants are grown. The third is that it is possible to lay straw on the pathways smothering weed growth and making them clean to walk on and work from; one can walk from the house to collect any produce without having to change one's shoes, which is a great help, especially for someone in a hurry to prepare a meal!

There is even a further bonus in that the beds, being 4 feet 6 inches (1.37 m) wide, with paths 15 inches (38 cm) wide, actually allow a greater cropping area, particularly for salad crops – lettuce, radish, spring onions and carrots. This may be contrary to what one may first suppose, but using orthodox methods the spaces between the rows must be wide enough for the gardener to walk between them. Not only is this a waste of space, but since Nature always endeavours to cover bare soil

quickly with growth of her own choosing, the excess space between the rows becomes overgrown with weeds, which then have to be removed or destroyed.

With measured garden beds and using the surface cultivation method, actual rows of vegetables, particularly, as mentioned, the salad type, can be grown with less space both between the rows and in the row, while spacing them only a little wider will allow the ground between the rows of salad crops to be used for a second, later sowing, to make a sort of intensive garden in

Picture 2   Strip beds that have been laid out, taking account of the aspect.

miniature. Root crops can also be sown more closely and recent official research has confirmed that many root vegetables benefit by this.

Making the Raised Garden Beds

In assessing which part of the garden is the best for some strip garden beds it is as well to bear in mind the actual aspect. Usually, these beds are laid out north to south for the obvious reason of giving each plant its fair share of light and sunshine (see picture 2). If this orientation is not possible, then it is in order for the beds to run north-east to south-west or even north-west to south-east. It is assumed that the proposed area is clear of weed growth, but should there be a fair quantity of weeds, whether annual or deep-rooted, then these need to be cleared away first before the beds and paths are marked out; simply follow the directions given in Chapter 3.

The beds should be 4 feet 6 inches (1.37 m) wide, with paths 15 inches (38 cm) wide. A grass service path 3 feet (90 cm) wide at one end or down the middle should be allowed for in the layout of the garden or allotment. There should be a 15 inch (38 cm) strawed path between the service path and the bed or beds beside it.

The next step is to measure, mark and cut out the paths for garden beds. Have two light-coloured lines, each attached to strong pegs pointed at one end, and at least 18 inches (45 cm) long. Use a spade to remove the soil from the proposed paths (the spade will not be used for any future cultivations). Spread the soil over the bed each side of the path being formed (see picture 3) except in the case of heavy soils, especially clay, which do not break down easily; with these, each spadeful of earth is placed along the centre of the bed (see picture 4). Here it is useful to have a third line, which can be positioned down the centre of the bed as a

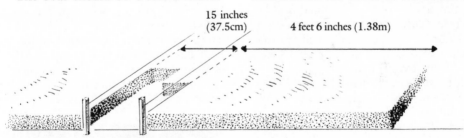

Picture 3   Soil from pathways is spread over on to the adjacent beds.

Picture 4   When the soil is heavy in texture, place each spadeful along the centre of the adjacent bed and spread it when it has broken down sufficiently.

guide to where to place the soil. Whatever the nature of the soil, try to resist turning it over when it is removed from the path; it should only be placed the same way up as before it was removed. Heavy soil placed along the bed centre will eventually break down later in the season, and can then be spread over the bed.

As the soil is being removed from the path – and this applies to either the light soils or the clays – firm the sides of the beds with the back of the spade. For heavy soils the path depth of soil to be removed needs to be 5 to 5½ inches (12.5 to 13.75 cm) and for lighter soils a depth of 4 to 4½ inches (10 to 11.25 cm) is recommended. After the soil has been removed the paths should be liberally covered with domestic soot to deter slugs – though, of course such soot is not always readily available in these days of gas and oil central heating and it may be only those living in rural areas who can obtain it.

Either way, the paths should next be spread with newish wheat straw. A standard rectangular bale will be sufficient to cover ten paths, each 18 feet (5.40 m) long (or the equivalent) to a depth of about 2 inches (5 cm). When the baler cords are cut, the straw will be found to be packed into the bale in wads. Remove one of these at a time and, holding it low to the ground over the path if the day is at all windy, ease out the straw to cover the path a few feet at a time. However, it is better to delay strawing paths if conditions are very windy. When strawing is completed, re-tie the baler cords around any straw remaining.

Straw varies in length, but the longer it is the better it will be for use on pathways. Always endeavour to obtain long wheat straw, as it will last longer than either oat or barley straw, although the last two are reasonable

alternatives. Most cereals are harvested by a combine harvester, and the resultant straw is rather short.

Besides providing clean underfoot conditions and acting as a weed smother, straw has a very pleasant appearance; it is a natural product and will thus help to create a pleasant environment in your garden or allotment.

If the garden beds and paths are formed in the spring period of the year and new straw is laid then, it will be found that this will last all the summer and into the autumn. As there is very little work during the winter – there is no digging to do – it may well be possible to delay putting down a fresh covering of new straw until the following spring; it all depends on conditions.

Cultivation without Digging

The Scrapper and its Use

Cultivation of the soil, whether on raised garden beds or in shrub and flower borders, is performed using a small hand tool we call a 'scrapper'. This is similar to an ordinary swan-necked onion hoe, except that it has a wider blade – 5 to 6 inches (12.5 to 15 cm). It is approximately 14 inches (35 cm) in

Picture 5 A scrapper.

length overall and weighs about 8 ounces (200 grams). (See picture 5.)

The name 'scrapper' appears to have originated from the Dutch market gardeners who came over to England between the wars to grow outdoor and indoor salad and culinary vegetables for the English market. They probably meant 'scraper', but 'scrapper' is how they pronounced it. The Dutch growers were not keen on weedkillers, so they used the 'scrapper' a great deal on their intensive holdings in the East Riding of Yorkshire when weeding between salad crops as well as for freshening the soil generally. In those days the idea of making use of weeds for composting was something new, so invariably the weeds were simply left on the ground to wilt or rot, depending on the weather and soil conditions. The veganic system of course makes full use of weeds for composting, and there are other benefits to be derived from them, as explained in Chapter 6.

It was during the time the Dalziel O'Brien family were pioneering and evolving the surface cultivation technique, however, that the real value of the scrapper was appreciated and it became the main tool for cultivation. For the average garden or allotment where the veganic system is practised, the scrapper is now essential for surface cultivation, weed removal and freshening of the soil on the non-compacted garden beds as well as any shrub or flower bed.

How to Use the Scrapper

The way the scrapper is held is of vital importance. For clearing weeds and crop debris, for freshening the soil and for the initial soil preparation prior to seed sowing, it should be held with the blade tilted down to the left and its lower point penetrating the soil to some 3 to 4 inches (7.5 to 10 cm) on the garden beds. This depth is critical as it

strikes a balance between cropping considerations and the development of the soil. Avoid allowing the blade to drop into a 'flat' position. True aeration is achieved in inturned soil. If the soil's own transformation is to take place in three to four years, it is unwise to disturb the soil unduly below 4 inches (10cm). In using this method of cultivation it will be found that the surface of the soil gradually raises itself to a higher level, meaning that the original soil is penetrated less and less as each successive stage is reached.

For a start it is best to practise on about a yard or so of cleared soil. Obtain a plank of wood 4 inches by 1 inch by 3 feet (10 cm by 2.5 cm by 90 cm) long and position it along the extreme edge of the bed, then kneeling, or half kneeling on it, hold the scrapper in the right hand and extend it over the soil to the centre of the bed (refer to picture 6). Tilt and insert the blade of the scrapper to the required depth and draw it smoothly back through the soil and along an imaginary line at 45 degrees to the path edge, finishing at the board. Repeat the stroke along the right-hand side of the previously worked soil, leaving no unworked soil between. Repeat until all the soil within

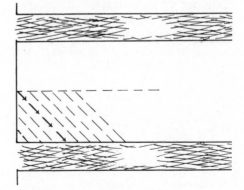

Picture 6 The arrows above show the direction of the first stroke when using the scrapper to cultivate the soil.

a comfortable reach has been cultivated, then work the uncultivated soil to the left of the original stroke (refer to illustration). Move the board to the right along the edge of the bed and continue working the soil in sections until all the bed is completely cultivated.

A surprising speed can be achieved with practice and a squatting position may be preferred to kneeling on the board, or making use of either whenever it suits. The board, however, does play a part in keeping the actual edge of the bed firm.

When using the scrapper for weed removal, again use the kneeling board, and hold the scrapper in the right hand and extend it over the soil at the same angle and approximate distance as before. As you pass the scrapper over the soil with the right hand to the place where it is to be inserted, reach out towards that point with the left hand and grasp any weed growth that has to be removed from the point at or nearest to the scrapper's insertion. Drawing the scrapper through the soil with the right hand, and pulling out the growth with the left, are simultaneous movements for the first pull out with the left hand, but whether or not there is growth where the scrapper is to be inserted, it must not interfere with the direction of the stroke of the tool, which is held at the same angle and takes the same direction as if it were clear soil.

Over the past forty years the scrapper has proved to be one of the handiest of garden tools, and because of its lightness and design children enjoy using it and become much keener to learn to do things in the garden (see picture 7) – weeding and giving the soil a gentle 'freshening' to name just two. The scrapper is a tool that all the family can use.

Picture 7   Children are more likely to enjoy helping in the garden when they are given a light tool that is easy to use like the scrapper.

CHAPTER 5

VEGANIC COMPOST MAKING, SEED SOWING AND PLANTING

Veganic Compost

Nature herself is reasonably intensive in producing a fresh form of growth immediately an existing one begins to decay, but this is too slow for the gardener. Therefore we need to know what to return to the soil, and also when and where in order to have humus readily available in a short period of time. There is nothing mysterious or magical about making rich, friable compost, just clear directions and a minimum of equipment. Veganic compost is particularly easy and quick to make and all plants thrive on it. It is clean, hygienic and free of disease, it rapidly converts vegetable matter into rich humus in a matter of weeks in the temperate zones, and from twelve to fourteen days in the sub-tropical and tropical zones. It renders heavy clay soils more friable with a much improved crumb structure. Lighter soils become more colloidal and moisture-retentive.

Veganic compost is applied to soils in less bulk when combined with surface cultivation. It is a major factor in producing fresh, healthy, high-quality vegetables and fruit of fine flavour, and it enhances the colour and fragrance of flowers. The main requirements are:

1. natural timber containers;
2. correct assembly of selected vegetable matter;
3. herbal activator to assist decomposition;

4. choosing the best site in a garden or allotment.

Compost heaps may be started at any time of the year as materials become available. With the veganic method, first heaps may well have to be made with materials from outside one's own garden, such as waste trimmings from greengrocers. Otherwise under normal circumstances vegetable trimmings, thinnings, raw selected kitchen waste and grass mowings (but not from roadside verges – they are full of rubbish) plus annual weeds will provide a good start.

If the garden or allotment is already under cultivation and has various vegetables growing, it is essential that all crop debris is removed from the soil's surface, and not left lying on it. This is because crop debris, whether left on the surface or buried, creates a perfect environment for pests and diseases, whereas any freshly pulled or cut growth is generally ideal compost material.

Materials for the Containers

Care needs to be taken when either making or buying containers, which should be of plain wood. There are firms selling compost containers (a supplier is given on page 139) and it is important to make sure they are left untreated, though a coat of stain on the exterior will enhance their appearance. Anyone in a position to make their own containers is referred to the dimensions for timber requirements in Appendix 2. Compost materials in direct contact with plain, untreated timber make better-quality compost; they also take the minimum time to break down and eventually mature. Wood may be expensive to buy, but if new timber is used then the life of a container ought to be ten years (see picture 8). 'Slab wood', the unseasoned trimmings from large tree trunks, is suitable, and relatively cheap. Avoid old wood which shows signs of rotting. Also avoid metal or plastic bins, polythene sheeting or bricks. In a very large garden, satisfactory bins can be made simply by making an enclosure with straw bales, 4 feet (120 cm) wide and as long as necessary. A cover should be constructed of timber.

Picture 8 A well-made compost bin that will last.

Positioning the Containers

If possible, site any compost containers close to the vegetable plot and as close to the kitchen as practicable. With veganic compost-making there are no flies and no unpleasant smells. At the same time, try and place the bins where they are not overhung by any large tree, and where they are out of the full sun. Don't put them in a place that can become waterlogged in winter. Generally speaking, a combined vegetable and soft fruit area of some 100 square yards (83.5 sq. m) will require two 3 feet (90 cm) square bins. Bins are always best in pairs, so that one is maturing while the other is being filled. This also saves wood (refer to Appendix 2). The photograph shows a twin bin, approximately 6 feet (180 cm) by 3 feet (90 cm) with a height of about 3 feet (90 cm) at the front with a cover of timber (plywood covered with roofing felt). Always stand the bins on clear garden soil. Before doing so, take off the top 3 inches (7.5 cm) of soil and pile it on one side; it will be used as soil layers in the first heaps and for topping them off when they are completed.

Materials for a Fine Heap

The materials for the fine heap will be mainly from the average home garden where vegetables are grown, plus any short grass mowings. Additional items include selected raw kitchen waste. Old straw is useful, but not essential.

Suitable materials include the following: vegetable trimmings and thinnings; crop residues (with a few exceptions); soft weeds – mainly annual, including grass weeds; very young docks; short grass mowings; green manures – such as tares; comfrey and various other herbs. Additions from the kitchen can include small quantities of fruit peelings, citrus fruit rinds and pulp, discarded fruit (uncooked) and banana skins. It is best for these to be cut up. Also suitable are flowerheads and leaves; tea leaves though not strictly 'raw' can be used, and the same goes for black coffee dregs. (It is reckoned that a saving of about 15 per cent in the volume of all refuse collected by local government refuse departments could be achieved, if households could compost vegetable and fruit waste. This would be a significant saving!)

These materials, assembled and treated with the herbal activator, will, in a 3 feet cube (90 cm³) sized bin, be ready for use in 4 to 6 weeks during the summer. Those with larger gardens and possibly having a bin or bins sized 4 feet (120 cm) by 4 feet (120 cm) by 3½ feet (105 cm) and who can confine a heap to soft annual weeds and short grass mowings, and provided always they use the herbal activator, will find that heaps take only fourteen days to mature during the summer period from mid-May to mid-September.

Assembling the Materials

The heap must, as mentioned, be made on clear soil; this is to encourage the entry of worms and bacteria which break down the materials and convert them into compost. Before building up the heap in layers (see picture 10) as the materials become available, a few short lengths of well-charred wood should first be placed directly on the soil base. The charcoal absorbs any impurities from the heap as it is assembled; the same pieces will suffice for three to four heaps.

The layers are now assembled as follows. First comes a 3 inch (7.5 cm) layer of old straw, if available. Otherwise begin straight away with what would be the next layer, i.e. a layer of green material about 9 inches (23 cm) deep. Any short grass mowings need to be mixed in with other green materials, or alternatively, a layer of them may be spread no more than 1 inch (2.5 cm) thick; otherwise they will remain as a matted wad, and will not decompose.

On this sprinkle water (about 4 pints per square yard, or, 2.75 l per sq. m) then a whitening of finely ground garden lime (not builders or slaked lime) followed by a thin covering of fine soil, from the pile which was placed beside the bins (about ½ an inch, or, 12 mm). Sprinkle the herbal activator solution (see page 30) on this cover of soil, using a quarter of a pint for each square (0.14 l per sq. m). Repeat this sequence until the container is full. To complete the heap, cover it with a final topping of soil 1½ to 2 inches (4 cm to 5 cm) thick. There will be some sinkage of the heap after a few days – this is to be expected.

Always keep a wet hessian sack on the top, to prevent the damp heat from escaping. It is also essential to have a water-proof lid over the entire bin to keep out rain, and this should always be in place during wet weather. Experience will determine the degree of moisture needed within the heap; it must not be too wet or dry.

The great advantage of this type of vegetable compost-making is that it does not require any turning. The compost will be ready for use when it has become loam-like in texture, resembling a rich, moist soil. If there is more of the garden down to soft fruit than vegetables, then mulches of semi-mature compost can be applied before this stage is reached, when the materials are unrecognizable, but not yet transformed into compost. Where vegetable (or flower) seeds are to be sown, only fully mature compost should be used

As mentioned, an average summer heap will take four to six weeks to mature. An autumn one will take around eight to ten weeks, and a winter heap completed during November could be ready for early March sowings and plantings.

Sorting out raw kitchen waste mate-

Picture 9   Mature veganic compost.

rials soon becomes second nature once organized. With an average family of four, it will be found that two or three bucketsful of vegetable and fruit waste can be available each week. Well-made veganic compost is sweet-smelling, pleasant to handle and completely disease-free. In addition it is an ideal culture medium in which beneficial micro-organisms proliferate.

After-care of the Maturing Compost Heap

Anyone attempting to make compost for the first time may discover that the fine heap has not matured in the manner described. Skill comes with practice, and early success will be made

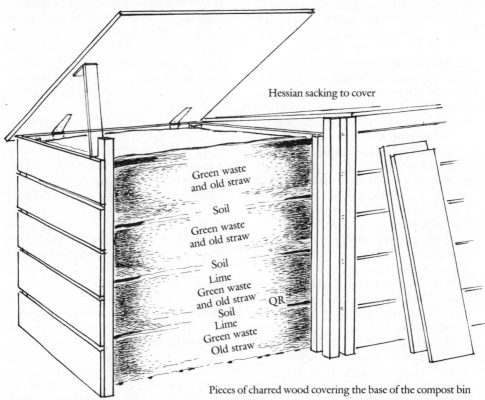

Hessian sacking to cover

Green waste and old straw

Soil

Green waste and old straw

Soil
Lime
Green waste and old straw
Soil
Lime
Green waste
Old straw

QR

Pieces of charred wood covering the base of the compost bin

Picture 10   Order of assembly of compost materials
(*Note*: it is important to sprinkle QR herbal activator only on the soil layers.)

more likely by observing the following points:

1. Ensure that the heap is always warm and damp, but not saturated. If the heap is at all soggy and smells unpleasant, it needs air. When building up a heap it is important that the materials are never pressed or trampled down. So simply loosen the heap with a fork (the heap must not be turned) and reactivate with the herbal activator solution in the following way. Make four or five holes with a broom handle, spacing them equally. Push the broom handle down to within 6 inches (15 cm) of the ground. Pour an equal amount of the solution into each hole. Add fine soil, working some of it into each hole.

2. If the heap is dry and grey with a powdery mould, loosen it, add fine soil, reactivate with herbal activator and drench with compost solution (a trowel of ripe compost to a gallon (4.5 l) of water).

3. During assembly, it may be found that the materials are on the dry side, in which case sprinkle them with water; and always keep the damp sack already mentioned on the top of the actual heap, as damp heat escapes rapidly. It is important to retain the damp heat as bacteria increase more rapidly at high temperatures, so the need for a protective cover during assembly is essential. To test the state of the heap near the time when it ought to mature, simply take out a trowelful of the compost; if it smells sweet and there is an absence of earthworms then it is ready.

Unsuitable Materials for Making Fine Heaps

Coarse roots and the woody stems of brassicas are unsuitable for fine heaps.

Unsuitable for any heap are the haulms, tubers and peelings of potatoes; stems, leaves and roots of rhubarb; sawdust, vacuum cleaner dust; cooked food; animal excreta, excessive amounts of either windfall apples, plums and acid fruits or citrus fruit peelings and rinds; and tree leaves, which should be reserved for the tree leaf compost (see page 30). So far as potato haulms, roots and tubers and/or the leaves, roots and stems of rhubarb are concerned, these are best burnt and the resultant ash used as fertilizer; otherwise, dispose of them with the household rubbish – they cannot be turned into good compost. Only very old weed seeds will be destroyed in veganic compost. Most weed seeds survive the heat generated in any heap. Therefore seeding weeds should be either burnt or disposed of with the household rubbish. Flowering weeds can go in the heap.

Rough Heap Materials and Assembly

A feature of the veganic system is the type of compost required, especially in the first year if there is likely to be a preponderence of deep-rooted weeds and creeping weeds, such as couch, etc. This is where the rough heap differs from the fine heap compost used for seed sowing and plantings. The compost from the mature rough heap (see picture 9) is used to provide soil layers when building up fine heaps. The rough materials have thus gone through a double decay process.

The rough heap can include coarse woody stemmed weeds, brassica stems, surplus grass mowings and old straw. Rough heaps are, of course, only required if the garden is an extensive one or a large allotment – and so will only apply in either case if the garden or allotment is badly overgrown with a high proportion of deep-rooted noxious weeds.

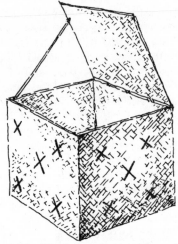

Picture 11 **Making a wire netting and straw box.**

You need a piece of wire netting (½ inch, or, 12mm mesh) 15 feet by 6 feet (4.6m by 1.83m) and some clean, new straw.

To make the lid, cut 3 feet (90cm) in from the end of the netting, so that you have a piece measuring 3 feet by 6 feet (92cm by 1.83m). Fold it in half to make a square, sandwich a 1½ inch (40mm) layer of straw between the wire netting halves and fasten the three open sides with short lengths of wire or string.

To make the box, fold the remaining netting in half lengthways and, as for the lid, sandwich a 1½ inch (40mm) layer of straw between the halves of wire netting, fastening the open sides with string or wire. Then fold it every 2 feet 9 inches (84cm) or so to form the box and fasten the corner to make a rigid shape. Sew through the sides with wire forming a kind of cross stitch to stop the sides bulging outwards. Then simply attach the lid to the box along one side, making the 'hinges' from slightly loose loops of wire or string.

In this situation, a wire netting and straw 'box' is easily made to house the 'rough' heap materials. (See picture 11.) Alternatively make a bin of straw bales as already mentioned. After the first year, there ought not to be any deep-rooted weeds to contend with, and any which may have been missed can be easily removed and burnt.

The assembly of a rough heap is the same as for a fine one, except that hard, woody stems need to be cut or chopped up prior to inclusion in the heap; you will need to remember, of course, to add a sprinkling of water and a whitening of garden lime, followed by soil and herbal activator, in the same sequence as for fine heap assembly.

Should there be excessive amounts of grass cuttings – and often there are – these need to be well mixed in with the chopped up material and any old, semi-decayed straw available, otherwise a thick wad of matted grass will soon form 'silage', which gives off a very unpleasant smell and will not decompose.

On opening up the rough heap, which may well be in about three months, it will be found that most of the original hard stems of brassicas and coarse weed roots are only partially decayed, while the remainder of the materials have broken down reasonably well. In this condition, rough heap compost is for use as soil layers in fine heaps, as any partially decayed stems will have virtually broken down completely by the time the fine heap is mature.

Green Manure Crops for Composting

If space permits in a garden or allotment, it will pay, in the first year, to have a small section down to growing green manure crops for additional compost material. Tares (vetches) are recommended and may be sown broadcast and raked in on a section of the garden or allotment free of crops for a period. Sown in late spring and summer, they quickly grow to about 9 inches (23 cm) high. A late summer sowing, given a fine autumn, will grow to around 9 inches (23 cm) in height too. Tares can either be cut down to ground level with garden shears, and allowed to grow on again to be finally pulled out completely, or else pulled up to start with, depending on the time the plot is occupied by them. Tares can also be sown in rows 2 inches (5 cm) apart; make shallow drills about 1 inch (2.5 cm) deep, hand place the seeds 2 inches (5 cm) apart, cover and lightly firm. Mustard is not recommended.

Converting New Straw into an 'Old' Condition

If new straw is incorporated into a compost heap, it will simply retard the rotting process, instead of assisting it. Should there be a problem in obtaining old straw for use in the heaps, the following method is useful in breaking down new straw. Separate the required amount of the bale on the ground and sprinkle it with prepared herbal activator, at the rate of half a pint (0.28 l) to a quarter of a bale. Thoroughly moisten the straw with water, and repeat the watering after a week. Allow at least fourteen days for the straw to attain a suitable state, though the average time for this is about three weeks. To hasten the process, chop the straw with a spade. The straw is ready for use when the 'varnish' has gone.

As the routine becomes established, a quantity of old straw becomes available from the strawed paths between the strip garden beds. This straw can be used as layers or mixed in with ingredients in subsequent compost heaps.

Compost Water; Seaweed Solution; Soot Water; Grass Water

To make compost water, take a double handful of compost, i.e. as much as may be comfortably held between the hands, put it in a 2 gallon (9 l) bucket of water and leave overnight. Provide a cover. Use within two days.

There is an excellent natural seaweed in soluble form (pure Maxicrop) available on the market as a concentrate to be diluted. It is invaluable when there is no compost ready and when starting the veganic routine. It should be noted though that soil structure will only improve permanently when the veganic system is adopted as a whole.

Dilute the Maxicrop seaweed concentrate at the rate of 1 teaspoonful (5 ml) to a litre of water, which nearly enough corresponds to 9 teaspoonsful (45 ml) to 2 gallons (9 l). Use as directed in the instructions for individual crops described in the book.

For soot water, fill a 1 lb (454 gram) jam jar with old soot, empty into a 2 gallon (9 l) bucket of water and cover; leave for twenty-four hours, but use within a week.

For grass water, soak half a bucket of soft, short mowings in 2 gallons (9 l) of water in a bucket and cover; leave for twenty-four hours, and then use within three days.

Tree-leaf Compost

Many gardens, especially in rural areas, have either a number of mature trees and hedges surrounding them or else one or more specimen trees or shrubs. In autumn there is usually an accumulation of leaves, and these can be turned into a compost which will benefit many shrubs and flower borders.

For this, a simply constructed wire netting container can house most deciduous tree and shrub leaves, along with surplus grass mowings and herbaceous flower debris. Omit rose prunings as the thorns never break down sufficiently to be softened, and also the hard shiny leaves of laurel and the acid leaves of horse chestnut.

Build on a clear soil base, and start off with old straw – if available – or, alternatively, begin with leaves and grass mowings and/or flower debris mixed well in. Add soil and the herbal activator, and repeat the sequence until a height of at least 3 feet (90 cm) is reached. To get the best results keep the heap covered against heavy rain.

A certain amount of soft hedge trimmings can be included in the mix, but any hard wood is best burnt along with the laurel and horse chestnut leaves and the rose prunings, and the ash used as fertilizer. This type of heap will obviously take longer to decompose; when the compost is ready, use it round flowering shrubs and flowers and any special ornamental tree. (Reserve the 'fine' heap for the vegetable and soft-fruit section.)

The Herbal Activator

The herbal powder is highly concentrated and is made up into solution form as required, preferably using rain water. Otherwise, tap water will do. Measure out a level teaspoonful (5 ml) of the powder and mix with a very small amount of water in a glass or cup to the consistency of thin cream. Add this to a pint of rainwater or tap water, cork up, and shake well. It is advisable to use a bottle with a cork rather than one with a metal cap. (An empty sherry bottle is ideal.) Keep the solution in the bottle for two or three hours before using – this is important. Try to plan it so that

this amount can be used within two weeks, as it must be sweet-smelling. If ever it smells a little off (sour), then discard it and make a fresh quantity. This herbal solution plays a vital role in the rapid breakdown of the materials in the compost heap, so it pays to take extra care when making it up. Label the bottle and store it in a cool handy place, and always remember to shake the bottle before using the solution.

As a guide, a quarter of a pint (0.14 l) of the prepared solution is sufficient for sprinkling on each soil layer in a 3 feet square (90 cm^3) heap.

The herbal activator is sold under the name Q R (Quick Return Herbal Compost Maker) and it is relatively inexpensive. Refer to list of suppliers, page 139.

Seed Sowing and Planting

Where vegetable seeds are to be sown, or plants planted, a mixture of mature compost, silver or sharp sand with some old domestic soot is made up in the following approximate proportions: about 5 pints (3 l) of soot, half a gallon (2.25 l) of sharp or silver sand, and about 6 gallons (27 l) of compost. These should be well mixed. Keep to the proportion of sand to compost whether the soot is available or not.

Large seeds have in the main com-

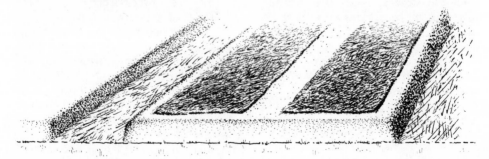

Picture 12 How seed compost is spread for the sowing of fine or very small seeds, such as radish, lettuce and so on.

post put along drills to a depth of about 2 inches (5 cm) and the seeds placed on the compost or just lightly pushed in to it, the soil being replaced and then additional soil drawn over to ensure that the seeds will be covered by 3 inches (7.5 cm) of soil; more detailed directions are given in the instructions on individual crops.

For the finer and smaller vegetable seeds such as lettuce, carrot, onion and radish, seed compost is spread over the surface of the soil twelve to fourteen days beforehand. This gives time for any weed seeds to germinate; the seedling weeds are then deterred from further growth by raking; only then comes the sowing of the vegetable seeds (see picture 12). Two gallons (9 l) of the seed compost will cover an area 3 feet by 1½ feet (90 cm by 45 cm); seeds are generally sown in 1½ foot (45 cm)

strips each side of the bed. (More detailed directions on individual salad crops are given in Chapter 8.)

Before the compost is spread the area must be moist, either through natural rainfall or from watering, or it will not become integrated and will get dried out.

When seed sowing, thinning or weeding, it is always a good idea to use a kneeling board (see Chapter 14 on tools and equipment) placing it along the edge of the garden bed (see picture 13). This will consolidate the bed edge, provide a clean surface on which to kneel, and ease the work and distribute one's weight more evenly.

When it comes to planting seedlings and large plants, and particularly at the beginning of the first season of adopting this alternative system, and possibly before the compost making has got into

Picture 13 Using a kneeling board when sowing seeds, a wooden marker to make the six drills and, in the foreground, a wooden presser.

its rhythm of supply and demand, an amount of compost can be put with each plant instead of spreading compost in a layer over the bed or section as described above for sowings. In this case, an extra mulch of compost will be required at an appropriate time during the plant's growth. Again, more detailed directions are given on pages 38–60, which cover vegetables, etc.

Plate 1 (*a*) This is how the allotment looked prior to being cleared

(*b*) This is how it looked two weeks later

Plate 2 (*a*)   A typical strip bed

(*b*)   Some veganically grown early carrots; the short tops are indicative of balanced growth

CHAPTER 6

A NEW APPROACH TO WEEDS

Just what is a weed is not easy to say, but the most common definition is 'a plant growing where it is not required'. Anyone with a garden or allotment is fully aware of how the weeds, if allowed to grow on, will have the effect of reducing the yield of vegetables or the growth of other plants, because of the competition for food, water and light between the cultivated plants and the weeds growing alongside. Such weeds have to be pulled or hoed out or destroyed by weedkillers.

However, in spite of these efforts to eradicate weeds, they will continue to emerge and grow each year because of the annual inversion of the soil by digging or ploughing. With the veganic system the soil goes through a natural progression in three years to the point where its fertility is vastly improved and there is a great reduction in the weed population. Followed correctly, the veganic system produces a condition where weeds virtually cease to grow.

The types of weed growth during a period of three full seasons indicate the three stages by which this natural conversion takes place. The first sees the deep-rooted types such as docks, thistles, dandelions, deep-rooted grasses and creeping grasses. The second may still see a few of the deep-rooted noxious type of weeds, but the main ones will be more surface-rooting types, such as groundsel, wild pyrethrum, scarlet pimpernel, fat-hen and tufted

grasses. The third and final stage weeds will consist mainly of finer and shorter species of grasses, along with chickweed, chamomile, nettle, wild pyrethrum and fat-hen, though less of these will appear. Despite a degree of overlapping during the three phases, each one is recognizable by the preponderence of the weed growth appropriate to it.

The Natural Way to Weed
In the veganic system of gardening there is more to weeding than simply pulling them up, though this is far more natural than using selective weedkillers to destroy them. The usefulness of surface-rooting weeds, though of a limited nature, in proximity to vegetable seedlings may be appreciated if, during weeding, those immediately adjacent to the growing vegetable seedlings, are removed and a 'band' of weeds between 4 and 5 inches (10 to 15 cm) wide, or even wider depending on which crop it is, is left between the rows, to grow on briefly before being finally removed. This achieves a fivefold purpose:

1. A miniature shelter belt is provided between the vegetable seedlings at a time when they need to be protected.
2. The soil is kept moist by shading, preventing it from caking, especially on heavy clays.
3. The force of heavy rain is broken

and soil is not splashed onto the vegetable seedlings.

4. The two-part weeding process spreads the actual work.
5. The fibrous roots of the annual weeds assist in creating a better crumb structure.

A good time for the first scrap-weeding is when the vegetable seedlings need to be thinned out. Make sure that the first weeding is approximately 1½ to 2 inches (4 to 5 cm) either side of the rows (this band weeding is really only practicable when crops are at 7 inches (18 cm) or more between the rows as there is too narrow a space between closer-set rows). The remaining bands of weeds are removed before they begin to rob the vegetable seedlings of food, water and light; the weeds are pulled when they are 2 inches (5 cm) or so high and certainly before they actually run into flower-bud stage. They can be pulled sooner if the actual vegetable crop is growing well.

Always remove all the weeds to the compost heap as quickly as possible, to avoid their wilting, as material for the compost heap needs to be fresh.

One soon comes to appreciate that weeds can be of great value as an ingredient of the compost heap; they are rich in minerals and readily break down to help create good humus.

CHAPTER 7

WATERING

No gardening system can succeed unless a water supply is available, unless, of course, the garden is in a semitropical or tropical zone, where there is usually adequate rainfall. For the growing of all salad crops and culinary vegetables, an ample water supply is essential. This also applies to soft fruits and, where rainfall is inadequate, to top fruits as well.

The full benefit of a well-made compost and other natural additions to the soil of a vegetable organic nature, together with natural minerals, cannot be achieved without such a supply of water.

The Hosepipe

Generally speaking, most people prefer to use a hosepipe, though this will depend on the size of garden and on the local councils in charge of allotments, where applicable. If at any time the soil is dry to a depth of one inch (2.5 cm) then most crops are in need of water; brassicas, celery and indeed potatoes need copious amounts of water around their roots as well as light overhead spraying with water.

It is a fact that potatoes need abundant water in order to crop well, as even if there has been a moderate rainfall, it is no guarantee that their roots have received sufficient. It is far better to continue watering even in a drizzle, as indeed do many commercial growers.

Hand watering for all plants should first take the form of a mist-like spray, using the thumb or forefinger over the end of the hose, and directing it onto the plants for only a few seconds. Remove the thumb, lower the mouth of the hose close to the soil, and move it slowly along the rows or around the plant as the case may be.

It pays to really ensure that vegetables and fruits do not suffer from dry roots, especially in those gardens which catch drying winds. To be certain of whether seedlings or plants require water, test the soil to a depth below 1 inch (2.5 cm) and this is probably the best indication. Obviously, if there has been no rain for some time then water will need to be given to most plants, soft fruit and, in a prolonged dry spell, top fruit.

Unless rain is imminent all compost mulches need to be 'watered in' to ensure the rapid assimilation of compost with a pre-moistened soil which results in a rapid increase of beneficial soil organisms. Obviously if rain is actually falling there is no need to do this watering of compost applications. In fact, this is another advantage of having permanent paths between raised soil beds because applying compost mulches or 'seed compost' to soils when gentle rain is falling can be carried out without trampling or damaging the soil of the garden beds.

Anyone new to gardening and using

a hosepipe for the first time would be well advised to keep it out of the sun when not in use, as the sun causes it to deteriorate and can make the first few gallons of water passing through it so hot that it scorches plants. It is always best to test the temperature of the water coming out of the hose before actually starting to apply it.

For hose-to-soil watering (often referred to as ball or surface watering), allow a moderate flow, passing the hose slowly along the rows. The pace can be varied from crop to crop; slower for carrots, beetroot, parsnip, white turnip, and lettuce when nearly mature; quicker for radish, vegetable seedlings and young growth generally.

When you need to stop watering and have to do this by yourself, have an empty watering can or bucket in the pathway to put the end of the hose in while you go to turn the water supply off.

Methods of Watering using the Hose

Hose-to-soil watering (ball or surface watering) is done by holding the hose in the hand some distance from the end, and passing it between the plants, or around plants such as tomatoes, cucumbers, etc.

Mist spray is usually at a higher pressure than hose-to-soil watering. It involves pressing either the forefinger or thumb over the end of the hose until the spray is just a fine mist which should be directed over and above the plants as the case may be.

Spray watering: a little less water pressure is required, and the thumb pressure should be correspondingly less, so that a coarser spray results.

Fan spray is achieved by squeezing the end of the hose fairly flat so that a fan-shaped sheet of water emerges. This method is mostly used when needing to water a clear area of soil in the open.

A Note on Sprinklers

There are many different sizes and shapes of sprinkler attachment available, and these may well be useful in certain situations, particularly if you need to mist-spray or fan-spray a given area for some length of time. Otherwise, it is a nuisance having to remove the sprinkler attachment after only mist-spraying a small area before hose-to-soil watering. It is also important to confine any sprinkling to the actual soil bed and not allow excess water to get onto the pathways, which is a waste of water, deteriorates the straw and encourages slugs, etc.

The Watering Can

In order to carry out any mist-spraying with a can, use a fine or medium type rose attachment which is easily removed for the ball watering or surface watering. Each of these is done by tilting the watering can to the required angle.

CHAPTER 8

OUTDOOR SALAD CROPS

Lettuces

There are many types of lettuce from which to choose, and there are varieties for sowing at different times of the year. The main types are cabbage, cos and looseleaf. The cabbage types are subdivided into two kinds – butterhead, which are mainly soft and round (see picture 14), and crisphead, which have crinkled or puckered leaves.

Picture 14 Rows of healthy round lettuces.

Among butterheads there is a wide choice, but Unrivalled is well known and reliable, with a heart of excellent flavour. Another good one with a more compact heart is All the Year Round. Among crispheads, Webb's Wonderful and Windermere are very reliable, while Tom Thumb is very early maturing with small, solid hearts. If you wish to grow cos lettuce then choose Little Gem or Lobjots Green. Little Gem is small and compact, with an excellent flavour. Neither it nor Lobjots Green need to be tied with raffia to stop their leaves from flopping outwards, but other cos lettuces may. Salad Bowl is a non-hearting, looseleaf type producing an abundance of fresh young foliage; its leaves can be pulled from the plants a few at a time.

Outdoor Sowing

Generally March is a good time to begin outdoor sowings; endeavour to sow at fortnightly intervals throughout the spring and summer for a continuous supply throughout the summer and autumn. For an average family it will probably be enough to sow three short rows at a time on one side of a bed to provide twenty-four plants plus some useful thinnings.

If the seed compost has been applied, as described on pages 30-31, at least twelve to fourteen days prior to the sowing day, then simply rake the composted area and with the back of the rake or the marking cane make ten to twelve ¼ inch (6 mm) deep indentations for the three rows, which should be 8 to 9 inches (20 to 23 cm) apart and running parallel with the path, the first 5 inches (12.5 cm) in from the edge of the bed. Try to sow as thinly as possible, say 2 to 4 seeds to the inch, and cover the seeds with ¼ to ½ inch (6 mm to 12 mm) of soil using the back of the hand. During the sowing and covering one can either squat in the path, kneel on the kneeling board placed along the extreme outside edge of the bed, or half-kneel, half-squat.

When the plants grow their first true leaves, they are thinned to 2 inches (5 cm) apart in the row, and any weed growth is removed from between the seedlings in the row and from a band of soil extending 1 inch (2.5 cm) either side of the row. Other weeds growing between the rows are left for the time being. Resist the impulse to make complete weed clearance. To help gauge the thinning distance, use the marking cane. Simply pull the thinnings and the weeds by hand without tools and place them straight into the weed box and thence onto the compost heap. No pulled-up green growth should be left on the soil or in it.

The second thinning takes place when the plants have grown enough for their leaves to touch one another. Remove the plants to a distance in the row of approximately 4 inches (10 cm). This time remove all the weeds and place them in the weed box as before. After the second thinning and weeding draw the point of the scrapper through between the three rows about 1 inch (2.5 cm) deep. This serves the dual purpose of slightly earthing up the plants and making a shallow channel along which the hose is passed in surface watering or the watering can in liquid feeding.

At this time also apply a mulch of compost, 2 gallons (9 l) to every 24 lettuces, and give them a liquid feed of diluted seaweed solution, ⅔ gallon (3 l) to every 24 lettuces, repeating the liquid feed every fourteen days. The repetitions of the liquid feeds are most important, as is watering: the soil must be kept moist at all times.

As the lettuces grow, take out every other one for table use. This will leave the remainder to mature at the 8 or 9 inch (20 cm or 23 cm) intervals. Lettuces normally take ten to twelve weeks to mature fully. Remember to keep the soil moist.

April and May are good times to sow the crisphead type, and the larger ones, Webb's Wonderful and Windermere, need rows 9 inches (23 cm) apart with 10 to 12 inches (25 cm to 30 cm) between the plants in the row.

Planting out Lettuce Seedlings

Lettuce seedlings raised from a sowing tray indoors can be planted outdoors in March and April providing the plants are well grown and have been hardened off. Plant the seedlings when the first true leaves are about the size of a thumbnail. (It is interesting to note that, other things being equal, the smaller the seedlings at planting time, the larger the lettuces at maturity.) Local nurserymen or garden centres may be reluctant to sell seedlings at the thumbnail size, but this really is the best size for planting outdoors, especially early in the year.

Again, have three short rows 8 or 9 inches (20 or 23 cm) apart, as for the sown ones, with the plants at 8 or 9 inches (20 or 23 cm) in the rows. Mark the rows the same way as making the seed drills, parallel with the path and the first 5 inches in from it. Or use a line. Either way use a marking cane for the plant distances. Have the container of compost at your left and the box of lettuce seedlings at your right. Make a hole with half a wooden clothes peg or suchlike, on the row mark or just beside the cane and a little deeper than you estimate the length of the seedling roots to be, then put in a small pinch of compost, about a thimblefull, and then the lettuce seedling. Give a slight pressure to the soil close to the seedling, and continue in the same way for the rest of the planting. Again make sure the lettuces are kept well watered and given liquid feeds as described above, plus a little more compost later on, if available. Remove any weeds which are in close proximity to the plants while they are in the early stage.

In the second season of the veganic system it may be possible to sow other salad crops between the lettuce, such as salad onions or radish, and this will be especially useful for anyone with a small garden and only limited space available. Another tip worth following is to sow or plant lettuces along the edge of a bed where peas or beans have been sown. Space the seedlings 8 or 9 inches (20 to 23 cm) apart in the single row and apply liquid feeds or compost water.

The watering of the peas or beans in the manner described for those crops will keep the lettuce in the right growing state, and the feeds ensure a steady growth and hasten maturity.

The aim should be always to keep up successive sowings of lettuces, as they are the basis of most salads, which form such an important part of nutritious meals for all the family.

Radishes

There are three main varieties of small radish: Globe for the earliest and latest sowings, French Breakfast to follow the earliest sowing of Globe, and a long radish – either red or white – for mid and late season. All varieties are sown in the same way, except the late ones. First sowings can begin as early as February outdoors followed by sowings at two-

or three-week intervals. Radishes can with advantage be sown along the edges of any garden bed which has been sown with peas or beans, but not brassicas. Six rows along, say, a 3 feet (90 cm) length garden bed will be useful for each successional sowing. This means the rows are 4 inches (10 cm) apart, with the last row 4 to 5 inches (10 to 12.5 cm) from the edge of the bed.

It is assumed that the seed-sowing compost has been applied twelve to fourteen days before sowing the radishes. Rake the area over to kill off any possible minute weed seedlings which may have germinated during the interval, though if the weather has been cold this is unlikely. In any event, rake the proposed area over and level it off.

Make a shallow v-shaped drill with either the edge-point of the scrapper or the back of the rake just less than 1 inch (2.5 cm) deep. Aim to drop the seeds ¼ to ½ inch (6 mm to 12 mm) apart as this will eliminate having to thin out. It pays to take a little more time to do this careful sowing. Actually it pays, too, to examine the seeds before sowing and discard the smaller and misshapen ones. After sowing, carefully push the soil over the seeds with the back of the hand or gently drag the back of the rake over the six rows. Firm the soil lightly with the presser board.

The radish section of a garden bed should be kept fairly moist, natural rainfall being supplemented by the surface watering method as described on page 36.

When the first rough leaves of the radishes are showing, it is time to take out any weeds, as well as any radishes that have inadvertently grown in a cluster, any faulty ones and the thinnings, and to put everything removed in the weed box and take it to the compost heap. At a ½ inch (12 mm) spacing the radishes will not need thinning; only where there chance to be several touching need any be removed. Use the scrapper to draw out a shallow drill along between the rows which will serve the dual purpose of slightly earthing up the radishes and making it easy for you to surface water with can or hose.

Begin pulling radishes for use as soon as they are large enough.

Autumn/winter radishes are large and can be grated in salads. Sow during the last week of June or early in July, as this will prevent them bolting. As the seeds are slightly larger than the Globe or French Breakfast types, aim to drop them an inch (2.5 cm) apart in the rows, thinning to about 3 to 4 inches (7.5 to 10 cm) apart when the first rough leaves appear. The actual rows should be 6 inches (15 cm) apart.

Liquid Feeding
Radishes are a crop which needs to be kept well watered and given at least two feeds of either compost water or diluted seaweed solution, one at the first-rough-leaf stage and another after fourteen days, at the rate of a ½ gallon (2.25 l) to a yard (90 cm) length of six rows.

Carrots
Early Carrots
The stump-rooted variety of carrot is the one recommended for the first sowing of the year. Of these, Early Market and Scarlet Horn are good choices.

Ideally, carrots like a sandy loam which doesn't dry out during the hot spells in summer. The soil should not be too stony and they need to be well watered during dry spells. Anyone anxious to grow good carrots will be pleased to know that they can be produced on most soils using the veganic system, and certainly the Minis-

try of Agriculture trials in 1975 and 1976 proved the point.

These early carrots are grown in exactly the same way as radishes, except that the rows are 5 inches (12.5 cm) apart. Always make sure the row next to the edge of the garden bed is 4 to 5 inches (10 to 12.5 cm) from the bed edge. The seed-sowing compost, which will have been applied twelve to fourteen days previous to sowing, is raked over; rows are marked by using the back of the rake to make shallow v-shaped drills, or else using the marking cane to make slight indentations. These depressions will need to be about ½ to ¾ inch (12 to 20 mm) deep; aim to sow the seeds very thinly, three or four to the inch, say. After sowing, carefully brush the soil over the seeds with the back of the hand or else draw it gently over using the back of the rake lightly across the rows. Firm with the presser board. Be sure to keep the soil moist; in extremely dry weather give a fine mist spray five days after sowing.

When the seedlings are about 1½ inches (4 cm) high, thin them out to 2 inches (5 cm) in the rows. The thinnings are pulled out, together with any weeds growing with them in the actual rows or in a band 1 inch (2.5 cm) wide either side. Other weeds are ignored at the first thinning, as with lettuce. Always choose a dull day to thin carrots, and be meticulous about removing all thinnings immediately to the compost heap via the weed box. It is very important not to leave any thinnings on the soil's surface as this attracts the carrot fly. After thinning, give a liquid feed of either compost water or diluted seaweed solution every ten to fourteen days, half a gallon (2.25 l) for a yard (90 cm) length of four or five rows. If you have any old domestic soot, it is a good idea to spread a fine film of soot over the carrot section.

When most of the weed growth is 2 inches (5 cm) high, remove all weeds by pulling. Use the scrapper to make a depression between the rows and along, as for lettuce. The soil should not be allowed to dry out during the growth of the carrots, and natural rainfall should be supplemented by surface watering at soil level along the depressions marked. Give also an occasional further over-head spray in a drought, choosing a dull period of the day.

Subsequent sowings of the same early varieties may be made as the carrots mature, but it is wise to sow a second batch, in any case. Carrot seed normally takes from fourteen to twenty-one days to germinate, depending largely on whether the soil at time of sowing was warm enough for germination. Expect carrots to be ready in eleven to fourteen weeks. Early varieties can be sown again in July and early August.

Maincrop

As maincrop carrots are potentially larger, both root and top, more space is required between the rows and between individual carrots at the final thinning. Space the rows at 8 inches (20 cm) apart and finally thin to 5 to 6 inches (12.5 to 15 cm) apart in the row. This will mean that on one side of a strip garden bed there will be three rows (see picture 15).

A good, rather long variety for maincrop carrots is New Red Intermediate and a popular stump-rooted maincrop is Chantenay Red Cored. The early weeding routine follows the same pattern for all varieties. Hand pull the weeds at all times. The first thinning and removal of weeds is as already described, again leaving any weeds in the middle between the rows to grow on. Give a liquid feed as for earlies and repeat at ten to fourteen day intervals. The second and complete weeding

Picture 15 Maincrop carrots need more space between rows as they take up more room above and below ground than do early carrots.

comes when most weeding of the weed growth is 2 inches high (5 cm). Again draw the scrapper along between the rows. The early varieties should not be weeded a third time, but the maincrop carrots may need to be, about five weeks after the second weeding.

During a dry spell test the soil occasionally in the way described on page 35 and for each overhead spray give three surface waterings along the depressions between the rows.

Carrots grown by the surface cultivation method will on average have larger roots in proportion to the amount of top than one usually sees. Smooth and well-shaped carrots will result if particular attention is paid to keeping the soil at the right moisture level.

Salad Onions

These are sown as described for radishes. They may also be sown on the same garden bed where peas or beans have been sown, as also suggested for radishes.

A good variety is the popular White Lisbon which has a silvery skin, mild flavour and grows quickly. Sow in succession from March to early May and then again in August or early September to overwinter if possible. When the weeds are about 2 inches (5 cm) high, remove by hand and then make a depression with the scrapper point about 1 inch (2.5cm) deep, in the same way as for other closely sown crops. The soil should always be moist for salad onions, and never allowed to dry out during growth. Natural rainfall should be supplemented by surface watering at soil level, by passing the hose along the depression between the rows. Choose a dull day for doing this if possible.

Give the onions at least three fortnightly liquid feeds of either compost water or seaweed solution at the same rate as for radishes.

Beetroot

Choose a good variety like Crimson Globe (see picture 16). In early April, prepare the soil with seed-sowing compost as already described on pages 30–31 and plan to sow first in the period mid-April to early May, when the soil has had a chance to warm up.

On the sowing date rake the surface. Beetroot can be sown in rows 5 inches (12.5 cm) apart for the first sowing, and 8 inches (20 cm) apart for the second. As with carrots the seeds are sown ¾ inch (20 mm) deep, with 3 inches (7.5 cm) between them, the marking cane being banded at 3 inch (7.5 cm) intervals. Each beetroot seed is in reality a cluster of seeds, so one every 3 inches (7.5 cm) should be adequate. Brush enough soil over the seed with the back of the hand to fill the drill, and water three days after sowing.

Picture 16   The beetroot variety 'Crimson Globe'.

When the beetroot have two true leaves each, thin by removing all but the most superior; this is usually the sturdiest in appearance, but do be sure to check that it is a normal one and not 'blind', that is, with no growing tip and so unable to develop. The watering and weeding routine is the same as for carrots. The scrapper is not used for removing weeds, but is used when the soil is cleared by inserting the left-hand point and drawing it through the soil to a depth of 1 inch (2.5 cm) in the centre between the rows.

Tomatoes

Of all the vegetables grown today, the tomato is one of the most popular. Home-grown tomatoes produced without digging and using veganic compost are a must for everyone with a garden, and flavour is greatly enhanced.

Select a position with plenty of sun, whether it is a south-facing border or a strip bed in the home garden or on the allotment. It is essential for tomatoes to be protected from cold winds, as they flourish best in a warm, sheltered environment.

If you are unable to raise plants from seed, then purchase well-grown plants from a horticultural nursery or garden centre. Endeavour to buy only those which are sturdy, healthy and without discolouration of leaves. Only buy tomato plants which are in individual containers. Of the upright growing tomatoes which are recommended the following are good and reliable:

Moneymaker. Probably one of the best; a widely grown tomato, with fruits of medium size and pleasant flavour.

Ailsa Craig. Uniform, medium-sized fruit and very good flavour.

Alicante. A popular variety, rather like Moneymaker, maturing early and producing a good crop of medium-sized fleshy fruits.

Outdoor Girl. Fairly early ripening, with dull red small fruit. The bottom truss may have anything up to thirty tomatoes. The flavour is fair.

If you have a greenhouse and/or the time to grow plants from seed then refer to Chapter 12 for growing under glass.

The first week or two in June is the best time to plant out of doors, as the danger of frost is over. Allow 14 inches (35 cm) between the plants in the row, and at least 12 inches (30 cm) from the edge of the garden bed. This will ensure ample space for root growth.

Make a hole large enough to accomodate both the plant root and a double handful of veganic compost. Make sure the seedling leaves of the plant are just above the soil level after firming round each plant. If the area has recently been lawn the soil round the stem must be firm or it may harbour wireworm. For supports use either a bamboo cane or

smooth timber stake (not a hefty one) and use raffia to tie each plant to stake or cane. Tie in a loose figure of eight, one loop round the stem and the other round the support, and finish with a bow on the cane or stake

Give a liquid feed of diluted seaweed solution and repeat every ten to fourteen days; dilute at the rate of 6 teaspoonsful (1 capful) (30 ml) of the concentrate to 6 litres of water. This will be sufficient for six plants.

When the first truss has formed – that is when the tomatoes are the size of blackcurrants – apply a mulch of veganic compost to the soil round each plant, at the rate of a 2 gallon (9 l) bucket of compost to six plants. Be sure to water the soil round each plant before applying the mulch. Repeat later, in July. It is essential to pinch out the tiny sideshoots which appear between the main single stem and the intersection of the leaves to ensure a strong main stem. This is best done when the sideshoots are an inch (2.5 cm) long. Basal suckers must also be removed if they occur. Continue to tie the plant to the support during its growth.

Anyone living in the north of England – even in a sheltered position – can expect only three good trusses of tomatoes to develop, and those in the south can expect four trusses. Generally the first ripe tomatoes are ready for picking in about the third week in August, but obviously the weather determines this.

Outdoor Ridge Cucumbers

For growing ridge cucumbers successfully outdoors a sheltered garden is really needed and protection against cold winds ought to be provided. A really good variety is the Burpless Tasty Green as it grows well and produces heavy crops. The fruits are at their best when about 9 inches (23 cm). They are tolerant of summer heat. Seed may be sown outdoors from mid-May to the end of the month and it is best to sow them where they will actually grow. Otherwise most garden centres or horticultural nurseries have plants available, usually from about the first week in June.

If you decide to have more than one plant see there is at least a gap of 2 feet (60 cm) between them. Choose a warm sunny position, and using a garden fork, make a hole on one side of a garden bed and approximately 18 inches (45 cm) in from the edge, large enough to accommodate about two-thirds of a gallon of compost, as well as the plant root if you are planting out. After planting make a slight mound so that during watering the water will percolate quickly into the soil and not stay around the main cucumber stem;

otherwise there is always the danger of stem rot. If you are sowing *in situ,* sow three to four seeds on edge ½ inch (12 mm) deep, in the centre of the mound, 2 inches (5 cm) apart. When the first true leaves appear remove all but the strongest plant.

When six or seven true leaves have formed, pinch out each growing point to encourage the production of sub-laterals. Give a mulch of compost to the soil around each plant every three or four weeks, a gallon (4.5 l) to each plant, making sure the soil is moist before applying it. Ten to fourteen days later, and at similar intervals thereafter, liquid feed the plants with 3 litres per two plants of seaweed solution. It is essential to keep up the watering, especially in dry hot periods. Gather fruit when mature, as production soon falls if many over-mature fruits are allowed to remain on the plant.

CHAPTER 9

VEGETABLES

Broad Beans
Main Sowing

A very early start can be made in late October or early November (see below), but the best time is probably the early spring if the soil and weather conditions allow a sowing in late February or March; the soil has to be free of frost and not too wet.

There are white and green-seeded varieties, and one of the most popular is the white-seeded Exhibition Longpod, which has pods of good length each containing between seven and nine beans of excellent flavour. Another reliable variety is Imperial White Windsor. Green-seeded varieties are Green Windsor and Masterpiece Longpod. For very small gardens or those exposed to high winds, try one of the dwarf types such as the Sutton. This variety can be sown in April.

Half a pint of seed will be just right for a 20 foot (6.1 m) row. If the beds were formed over the winter and there is any unwanted green growth on the strip garden bed, it is removed by using the scrapper and put on the compost heap.

Begin by placing a marking line in position 20 inches (51 cm) from the edge of the bed, hammering or pushing the pegs in firmly so that the line is about an inch (2.5 cm) or so above the soil, and it is taut. Make a drill 9 inches (23 cm) wide and 4 inches (10 cm) deep, standing in the path, and drawing the soil out from the line towards the bed edge. Make sure the drill is an even 4 inches (10 cm) deep. Spread veganic compost along the flat drill at the rate of two 2 gallon bucketsful of compost for a 10 foot (3 m) row. The bean seeds are just pushed into the compost 9 inches (23 cm) apart in three staggered rows, the two outer rows being at the edge of the drill. Cover the seeds by drawing the soil from the drill back over them, forming a slight mound. If the soil is a loamy or sandy type, lightly firm with presser or with the back of the rake. Finally liquid feed with veganic compost water or diluted seaweed solution at a pint per foot of row (2 l per metre). Repeat at ten to fourteen day intervals.

When the beans have grown 9 to 12 inches (23 cm to 30 cm) high, give a mulch of compost along the entire length of row at the rate of 2½ pints per foot of row (4½ l per metre). Be sure to water the soil before applying the compost mulch.

A later sowing can be undertaken towards the middle of June, and the variety recommended is Green Windsor. In this case use two marking lines, one 10 inches (25 cm) from the edge of the bed and the other a further 10 inches from this line into the middle, each 1 inch (2.5 cm) off the ground. This makes a 10 inch (25 cm) wide space between the two lines which must be cleared of any weed growth.

This time spread mature compost

along the surface of the soil between the two lines. No drill is needed, and the planting knife is the only tool used for planting. Place the three rows of beans along the composted strip – the same distance and spacing as above. Take up a bean, having noted its exact place on the compost, and insert the planting knife 4 inches (10 cm) into the soil in the same place; withdraw it and drop the bean in the hole, then push compost over and give a slight press with the hand to ensure complete covering of the bean. After planting remove the marking lines and spread a fine film of soot over the composted strip. Surface watering is required after three days as June is normally a very dry month. When the beans are through, give a liquid feed of veganic compost water or diluted seaweed solution at the same rate as above and at the same interval of time. During growth water when necessary by overhead sprays as well as soil-level watering at low pressure.

When the earliest-sown beans have finished cropping, and, if the area is not needed for any other crop, then a secondary crop of beans may be obtained by cutting down the original haulms to within an inch (2.5 cm) of the ground. This will bring forth new growth from the roots, which will provide a further quantity of beans. (Frequently, fresh growth starts from the roots before the first haulms have finished bearing; leave this to grow on to fulfil the purpose just described.) After cutting down, hand pull any weeds from the whole bed and firm the soil around the bean roots finishing with a film of soot over the ground.

Autumn-sown beans

Sowings may be made in late October or early November, but success will depend on favourable soil conditions at sowing time and on a fairly mild winter.

A good and reliable variety for such an early sowing is Aquadulce (white-seeded). Sow as for February–March, and feed likewise. It is important to keep an eagle eye out for the first signs of blackfly, particularly on the main crop – late February and March or even April sowings. If any is seen, smear soap and soot on the top young growth and leaves of the plant – both upper and lower surfaces – preferably during May. Spraying strong soapy water on the broad bean plants and stem is useful too. In any event, break off the tip of the main top shoot when the first bean flowers on the plants are setting tiny pods. This encourages bearing.

Picture 17   Some home-grown peas ready for picking.

Peas

Fresh home-grown peas (see picture 17) are a must for any family with a garden or allotment. There are many varieties to choose from. Peas are divided into two groups: round-seeded and wrinkle-seeded, or marrow-fat. The latter generally have the better flavour.

Of the early ones, Kelvedon Wonder

and Little Marvel are the wrinkled type. Another good early is the dwarf Feltham First; this is a round-seeded and is one of the earliest. An excellent second early is Onward (wrinkled); for a maincrop choose Senator (wrinkled) which gives a heavy yield. Half a pint (0.28 l) of peas will sow a 10 foot (3 m) row, and the preparation for sowing is the same as described for broad beans, although the manner of actually sowing the peas differs. Sow the peas by broadcasting them along the composted drill, making sure they are fairly evenly distributed. Draw the ridge of soil back over the peas, and lightly firm with a presser or the back of a rake.

February and March are two good months for sowing the early varieties, with March and April for the second early. Maincrop peas can be sown in April or May. A summer sowing of earlies, Kelvedon Wonder or Little Marvel, can be made during the month of June.

Generally speaking, it is better to give some support to peas, either with pea sticks or short lengths of bamboo. Even the dwarf types are better supported in order to keep the pods clean.

Weeds are removed by hand pulling with the aid of the scrapper (scrapweed) when the peas are about 6 inches (15 cm) high, and, with the dwarf and early varieties not again during the cropping season. After weeding give the peas a soak with water and apply a mulch of compost at the same rate as for broad beans and give liquid feeds of compost water or diluted seaweed solution every fourteen days. The peas should never be allowed to dry out at the roots.

Other varieties include Oregon Sugar Pod, a fine sugar pea (mangetout) reaching a height of about 4 feet (1.2 m). Sugar Snap has fleshy pods and is stringless when young; it can be used as sugar peas when either small or mature, although the older pods will need stringing. Alternatively the peas may simply be removed from the pods in the usual way when mature. Sugar Snap need to be well supported as they reach a height of 6 feet (1.8 m) or more.

Shallots

These are one of the first crops to be planted in the year, and may often be planted in February, otherwise in March. If there is compost ready, clear the proposed shallot area (three short rows along one side of a bed should be sufficient unless a large quantity is to be grown for pickling), then apply seed-sowing compost as described earlier. Leave for fourteen days and rake well.

Set the shallots in rows 9 inches (23 cm) apart, at 9 inches (23 cm) in the row. Place the bulbs in the soil, leaving the larger part uncovered. Use the planting trowel rather than pressing them in, as this is kinder to the base from which the roots will grow, and will also discourage them from rising up in the soil. Birds and even mice also pull them out, so keep checking them until they are well established.

Liquid-feed at planting and every 14 days, using compost water or dilute seaweed solution at the rate of half a gallon (2.25 l) to every twenty-four shallots. Weed carefully around the shallots to avoid damaging the bulbs. Keep the soil moist, but withdraw water once the foliage starts to die off in order to encourage ripening. Shallots are harvested in late June or July when the tops wither and die. Lift, separate and store in a cool airy place.

Onions from Sets

By far the most convenient way of growing large, ripe onions is from sets. Untreated bulbs may be put in the ground from the second week in

February but those that have been heat-treated (the general rule today) must wait till late March or early April. The heat treatment discourages bolting. Prepare the gound exactly as for shallots, although the area will probably be much more extensive. Plant the onion sets at the same distances – 9 inches (23 cm) between and in the rows – but rather deeper than shallots, so that only half an inch (12 mm) protrudes above the surface. Again, like shallots, they tend to rise and will need to be reset, perhaps several times. Birds and mice also like to pull them up.

Liquid feed the onions at planting and continue as with shallots. Keep the ground moist to encourage steady, even growth, and larger, riper bulbs; if the bed dries out the plants will stop growing, then when watered they will put on a spurt and become too lush or split. Again, weed carefully round the growing bulbs to avoid damage to them.

To ensure the best-ripened onions and hence the longest-keeping, it is worth taking some pains. Stage one in the ripening shows itself as a slight withering of the stems. Remove soil from round the bulb using the scrapper. Stop feeding, but continue watering as normal. Stage two is when the majority of the plants show withered stems; twist them half a turn at the neck of the bulb and turn the whole stem flat towards the north. Stage three comes a week later (not less) when the whole bulb is levered slightly out of the soil. Stage four comes after one more week when watering is finally stopped. Finally, lift when the foliage is completely brown and withered. Sun-dry. Store in a cool dry place.

French Beans
Dwarf French beans are vigorous plants, producing plenty of well-flavoured stringless pods over a long period if picked regularly. Of the early-maturing varieties, Tendergreen and Sutton's Masterpiece are two good croppers. Delicious too is the golden type Kinghorn Wax which produces fleshy pods, and another stringless variety, Sutton's Sigmacropper.

The best time for sowing the seeds of dwarf beans is the month of May. Assuming the ground is clear of weed growth, begin by marking three rows 9 inches (23 cm) apart on one side of the garden bed, with the first 7 inches (18 cm) in from the edge.

Use the marking cane for measuring the distance between the seeds or plants. It is better to place the beans on the soil close to the marking lines first, the beans being 9 inches (23 cm) apart in the row. Use the planting knife to make holes 3 inches (7.5 cm) deep. Then place a small handful of seed compost in the hole and drop in the bean, followed by another small handful of compost. Draw a little soil over to make a slight mound and press lightly with the back of the hand. Continue the same routine to complete the sowing. After two days, surface water unless heavy rain has fallen in the meantime. During the growing of the beans keep them well watered, and give a mulch of compost on clear moist soil, when the first tiny pods are showing, at the rate of 1½ gallons (6.75 l) per three rows 6 feet (1.83 m) long. Also apply a liquid feed of either compost water or diluted seaweed solution every fourteen days at the rate of 11 pints (6 l) to three rows.

Climbing French beans are making something of a come-back in popularity. They should be grown just like the dwarf variety but with a pole 8 or 9 feet (2.4 to 2.7 m) long inserted 1 foot (30 cm) into the ground beside each plant. The poles may be vertical and will not need to lean on one another except in

Plate 3 Tomatoes ripening in the sun; the variety is 'Moneymaker'

Plate 4 (*a*)   Firm, ripe onions

(*b*)   'Kelvedon Glory' sweet corn; two rows of plants are grown in a strip bed

the windiest gardens; then sow only a double row and support as runner beans, feed and water as the dwarf kinds. French beans, dwarf or climbing, do not much like to be transplanted and should always be sown where they are to continue growing.

Always pick French beans when they are young and tender. Not only will you pick better beans this way but you will also pick more by weight in the long run.

Be sure to compost the considerable amounts of French bean haulms immediately the first winter chill puts an end to harvesting.

Runner Beans

This popular vegetable is one of the exceptions to the general rule of growing in rotation with other crops, as the plants prefer to be grown on the same site year after year. It is well worthwhile to consider the siting of runner beans carefully as strong winds and summer storms can damage flowers and young beans. In common with the rest of the bean family, they need plenty of moisture and generous composting. Good colour and tenderness of pod as well as heavy cropping are then assured.

There are many good varieties from which to select, with Sutton's Achievement and Webb's Selected Scarlet Runner being just two

The normal sowing date is around 10–15 May, but in certain favoured areas it is possible to sow during the first week in May. The plants are tender and very susceptible to frost, so it pays to delay sowing to be on the safe side. There are various ways to sow runner beans, but a double row down one side of a garden bed is probably the best, as low-growing crops can be grown on the other side such as summer lettuce, which benefit from a little shade, especially during hot spells. Should

there be space at one end of the garden, and if this is a narrow strip that runs east-west, then this would be ideal as the beans would be facing south. Otherwise use the north-south aspect of the garden beds, but work out which would be the most suitable garden bed in relation to other strip beds in the garden or allotment, bearing in mind the different crops, etc.

Using a long hoe, take out a flat drill 12 inches (30 cm) wide and 2 inches (5 cm) deep. Spread 6 gallons (27 l) of seed-sowing compost along every 15 feet (4.57 m) of it. Then place the seed beans 10 inches (25 cm) apart in two rows – 8 inches (20 cm) between the rows – leaving a 2 inch (5 cm) space from each edge of the 12 inch (30 cm) drill. The soil originally removed to form the flat drill is then drawn back over the seeds, leaving a slight mound.

Supports

The supports are next put into position down each side of the double row of seeds. Unbranched hazel poles, bamboo canes or ¾ inch (20 mm) square battens 8 feet (2.4 m) to 9 feet (2.7 m) in length, one per seed, are ideal for the job. The usual method is to insert the poles or canes into the ground about 12 inches (30 cm) apart across the row and tilting them to cross one another about 18 inches (45 cm) or so from the top. In the v-trough so formed, a third line of canes or poles is laid horizontally, and these are tied to the other two at the points of intersection. Straining wires from the endmost canes to pegs driven in the ground will give reasonable stability. If space is short, then lash diagonal poles from ground level at each end to the crossing-point several poles along the row.

Two days after sowing, soak the sown area by surface watering, failing a heavy rainfall. Continue watering throughout the cropping season, as the plants must never be allowed to dry out. Spray the bean flowers with water to assist setting. When the first flowers appear, lightly scrap-weed the soil and remove any weeds to the compost heap; afterwards give a mulch of veganic compost along the whole length of the double row of beans at the rate of another 6 gallons (27 l) per 15 feet (4.57 m). Be sure to water the soil prior to mulching, unless it has just rained. Feed with seaweed solution and repeat every fourteen days or so at the rate of 1¾ gallons (8 l) of diluted solution to 15 feet (4.57 m) of row.

Instead of sowing bean seeds, you may prefer to buy young runner bean plants. In this case wait until the end of May or very early June, as any danger of frost should be over by then.

Use a small hand trowel or planting knife and plant each plant with half a handful of compost. Space them 10 inches (25 cm) apart in a double row along one side of the garden bed. Mulch, liquid feed and water as described above.

Leeks

Leeks respond extremely well to the no-digging and veganic composting routine, despite the fact that conventional planting instructions usually specify the digging in of animal organic wastes during the autumn or winter previous to planting.

Like carrots, leeks provide a good example of less work and less expense under a veganic routine and those grown in the newer way have a most delicious flavour. Whether you produce plants with a good 'girth' or slender is a matter of spacing in the rows.

Leek plants for planting out are easy to obtain, but even in a small garden or for an allotment it is recommended that seeds are sown in the open ground in the manner usual for small seeds (see pages 30–31).

The Musselburgh variety is a most reliable and proven one. Sow during March or April as soil conditions permit. Firm a small area on one side of a garden bed, mark three rows 20 inches (50 cm) long and 6 inches (15 cm) between the rows, and sow thinly two seeds per inch (2.5 cm) in a v-drill 1 inch (2.5 cm) in depth. After thinning to 1 inch (2.5 cm) apart when the seedlings are 2 inches (5 cm) high the seedbed should yield 60 leeks for planting out. By early June or July they should be pencil-thick. Water the seedbed the evening before the day for planting, and use a garden fork to lever out the plants to avoid breaking the roots; further care is needed to protect the roots from cold winds, so use a box and a cover. The best ones to plant are the most uniform-sized ones.

Planting

Select a garden bed where early peas or broad beans were grown. Mark three rows on one side of the bed, the first row some 6 inches (15 cm) in from the bed edge, with 9 inches (23 cm) between them. Use a marking cane to measure 9 inches (23 cm) between the holes, which should be made with a dibber 9 or 10 inches (23 cm or 25 cm) deep. Move the marking cane along as required, staggering the holes in the rows. Before actually planting the leek seedlings, trim the roots to prevent them pointing upwards when planting, and trim all the tops as well to the same length to ensure an even depth of planting; this also prevents the 'leaves' from drooping and being pulled down into the soil by earthworms.

Take up a handful of compost and drop half of it in the hole, then drop in the leek seedling, making sure the roots reach the compost at the bottom of the hole, then carefully put the rest of the compost round the leek. This ensures that the roots are anchored.

Avoid allowing soil to filter down as the leeks are dropped in, and endeavour to leave the hole open. Then carefully fill each hole with water, again avoid washing any earth from the sides of the hole in doing so. As the plants continue to grow, keep them fairly moist, never allowing the soil to dry out.

Freshen the soil when the plants are about ½ inch (12 mm) thick and give half a handful of compost mulch to each plant. Also draw some soil up to them. When the leeks are ready to use, lever them out of the ground using a garden fork.

Brassicas – Cabbage, Brussels Sprouts, Cauliflower, Broccoli, Curly Kale

All the brassica family can be raised from seed, without heat, by direct sowing into a prepared seed bed and then planted out into their final positions. A simpler way is to buy in plants from a reliable specialist nurseryman or garden centre. We shall deal first with the cultivation of ready-grown plants, and then describe how to raise one's own plants from seed.

At most garden centres brassica plants are on sale in small individual containers. Only buy if they are sturdy and healthy plants.

All varieties are planted in the same way, and receive similar attention during their growth to maturity. Any marked difference between varieties are explained below under separate headings. The main basic points for planting are:
1. Clear the garden bed by the scrapping routine.
2. Mark the rows with a line and use the marking cane for spaces between plants in the row.
3. Make a hole for each plant with the planting trowel and drop half a handful of compost into each hole, which must be deep enough to take the roots without doubling them, lower the roots into the hole – draw up the soil round the plant – making sure the lowest leaves are above the soil level – and finally firm the soil.
4. Surface water generously.

Brassicas need a fertile soil and plenty of moisture. Natural rainfall should be supplemented as necessary by hose-to-soil watering with an occasional overhead spray.

Another interesting and useful practice is to grow certain herbs between brassicas, especially dill (a hardy annual) and chamomile as well as sage and rosemary, which are perennial. These have beneficial effects on soil structure, assist in creating a sweet atmosphere around the plants and help in encouraging their growth. See also Chapter 10.

Give a compost mulch when those plants which need one are about one-third grown. Where plants were put in with a small amount of compost, give a more generous amount; a depth of 2 inches (5 cm) round each plant is about the right quantity, having first drawn up some of the surrounding soil to the stems of the plants. Remove any faded leaves and firm all plants around the stems. (The soil round brassicas must be firm at all times.) Subsequent application of compost mulches will depend on the soil's fertility and plant growth, but generally brassicas will need to be mulched at least twice, and sometimes three times during their growth. They should also be regularly fed with liquid feeds of either compost water or diluted seaweed solutions at intervals of between fourteen and twenty-one days, depending on the particular crop being grown, certainly up to October and resuming again in the early spring, where appropriate.

Always remove the roots of brassicas as soon as possible after cutting; the stems of brussels sprouts and kale are material for the rough heap, if you have one (chop up the stems before putting them on the heap).

It should be noted that animal dung spreads club root and probably many more diseases, according to the Ministry of Agriculture. So any infected root should be burnt and not put into a compost heap. This is another sound reason for growing brassicas from seed using veganic compost to ensure healthy plants from seedlings to maturity – given genetically sound seeds, of course. It is better to burn all brassica roots anyway: apart from being unsightly, they are serving no useful purpose left in the ground.

Where pigeons are a pest use tautly stretched netting at least 6 inches (15 cm) clear of the plants all round.

Although it is always tempting to 'buy in' brassica plants from the plant nursery or garden centre, raising one's own seed is far more rewarding, providing the young plants receive the attention they deserve. After all, they are to occupy perhaps a fair-sized area of the garden, some of them standing for nine or ten months, including January and February. Moreover, it also means that one can have exactly the varieties needed.

If you follow the instructions given below, the brassica seeds will become healthy sturdy seedlings fit for planting out at the correct time. And, having given them a good seedbed and adequate water, do resist the temptation to fill the space earmarked for planting them out in with 'more advanced specimens' seen in a local market or nursery.

Anyone very keen to have plants for setting out as early in spring as possible should sow Brussels sprouts, summer cabbage and summer cauliflowers in January or February, under glass, planting out in April or May or Hispi cabbage in late September to stand the winter under glass and be planted out in March. Summer cauliflower sown and planted at the same time as Hispi will usually be ready a little sooner than those sown in January or February.

In milder areas, particularly Devon and Cornwall, Brussels sprouts and savoys are often sown in the open in August, remaining unprotected in the seedbed till the following May, when they are planted out just like the plants from January or February sowings under glass. This method of course requires decent autumn weather for success and anyone living in these areas and wishing to try it is advised to seek local advice on suitable varieties, exact sowing and dates.

Seedbed Preparation and Seed Sowing

Given reasonable soil and seed compost being available, scrap-weed the proposed area and moisten the soil. Then spread a 2 gallon (9 l) bucket of seed compost over an area 3 feet (90 cm) by 18 inches (45 cm) on one side of a garden bed fourteen to twenty-one days before sowing seed.

Immediately after spreading the seed compost apply diluted seaweed solution (1 capful to 1¼ gallons (5.7 l) of water) using a watering can with a rose. Make sure the area does not dry out during the next fourteen to twenty-one days, then rake over well and make shallow drills 5 inches (12.5 cm) between the rows and ½ inch (1.25 cm) deep with the back of the rake. Sow all brassica seed thinly, aiming to drop the seeds ½ inch (1.25 cm) to 1 inch (2.5 cm) apart – they are large enough to do this. This will save a lot of thinning out and will ensure that each plant is sturdy. Cover with soil using the back of the rake or the back of the hand and firm with the presser board. Sprinkle a fine film of old domestic soot over the seedbed. After the third day, if there has been no rain, give a spray-water using the rose on the watering can. Thin the seedlings to 1½ inches (4 cm) to 2 inches (5 cm) apart when the first true leaves appear and give another liquid feed. Four rows in an area 3 feet by 18 inches (90 cm by 45 cm) will, after thinning, provide between 72 and 96 plants.

If you have a cold frame then this is a useful way to give the seedlings more protection during the early stages, but the glass will need to have been in place several weeks before sowing in order to take advantage of the warmer soil condition under a cold frame.

Cabbage

There are some varieties of cabbage which mature in the spring, summer, autumn and winter to provide a supply all the year round. The spring and summer types are the most succulent and flavoursome.

Spring Cabbage

Sow seed in July or August according to locality. When the plants are 3 to 4 inches (7.5 to 10 cm) tall – which will normally be from mid-September to mid-October – set them out in two rows on one side of a garden bed, spacing from 12 inches (30 cm) in the row, to mature the following spring – May to early June.

Varieties include:

Offenham Flower of Spring, with large and solid-pointed heads maturing April–May.

Harbinger, a very reliable one which has small pointed heads and few outside leaves.

Hispi, an F_1 hybrid, can be sown in autumn and overwintered under glass to be planted out in March.

Summer Cabbage

Seed is sown in April and plants are set out in May so that they are ready to cut in July and August (see picture 18). Again, like spring cabbage, set out two rows to one side of a garden bed with the same spacing of 12 inches (30 cm) in the row. Varieties include Golden Acre and May Express, which both make fine ball heads maturing eight to nine weeks from planting out. There are several varieties with pointed heads, including Greyhound and Winningstadt, which have a compact habit and solid-pointed heads, maturing August–October.

Picture 18 Summer cabbage.

Winter Cabbage

The main types are the savoys and drumheads, which are normally ready from October to January. They are grown in the same way and become very large. Taking longer to mature, they are not so succulent as the other kinds of cabbage

Seed is sown in April or early May and plants set out during May, June or even July, in two rows on one side of the garden bed, 18 inches (45 cm) between the rows and 18 inches (45 cm) in the row. Varieties include two of the hardiest and best, namely Winter White and Christmas Drumhead, which can withstand a severe winter. They mature during October to December.

The savoy is a wrinkled-leaf cabbage which also withstands severe frost without damage, and can be left in the ground until the new year, when winter cabbages normally finish.

Recommended varieties of savoy are January King, Ormskirk Rearguard and Aquarius (F_1 hybrid), similar to January King with a compact habit suitable for close planting.

Red Cabbage
This is grown in the same way as ordinary cabbage. For large heads, sowings can be made in July and August along with the spring cabbage sowings and plants set out from March onwards, in this instance 18 inches (45 cm) between the rows and 18 inches (45 cm) in the row, well firmed as with all brassicas.

Red Drumhead is a recommended variety.

Brussels Sprouts
Choosing the right two varieties will enable sprouts to be picked from about mid-September until spring.

For early picking, Peer Gynt, an F_1 hybrid should be sown in April, and transplanted out with approximately 14 inches (35 cm) between the rows. This will mean two rows on one side of a garden bed or four rows using the full width of bed, the first row being 6 inches (15 cm) from the edge of the bed. Having two rows on one side of the garden bed like this is only possible with Peer Gynt, as this is a dwarf variety usually growing only about 18 inches (45 cm) high, which makes it suitable

for small gardens. Firm sprouts will be ready for picking from October to the end of December, providing the ground is kept well firmed.

To follow Peer Gynt, try Perfect Line or Citadel F_1 hybrid or Roodnerf. All these will need to be sown during April and translated into their final positions in May or June. Set these varieties out at only one row each side of a garden bed and space them 22 to 24 inches (56 to 60 cm) apart in the row. Sprouts should be ready for use from December to March. If the garden or allotment is a very windy one it pays to stake each plant using a bamboo cane. The soil for growing Brussels sprouts needs to be fertile, and should be mulched at least once after planting.

Cauliflowers
Of all the brassicas, cauliflowers perhaps need most attention if they are to produce good-sized, solid, close and snow-white heads or curds.

Grown on a strip garden bed and given ample veganic compost together with seaweed solution through their period of growth, such cauliflowers should be possible, providing they are also given plenty of moisture especially in a warm and dry summer, as a starved and dry soil will not produce good-sized plants.

Late Summer and Autumn Cauliflowers
Sow seed thinly on a prepared seed bed – as for all brassicas already described – in rows 5 inches (13 cm) apart during March or April. By June the plants are ready to be put out in their final positions.

Plant the first row 7 inches (18 cm) from the edge of the garden bed, and the second row 18 inches (45 cm) from the first. Space the plants 20 inches (51 cm) apart in the row. Liquid feed at planting with either veganic compost water or diluted seaweed solution, ½ litre to each plant every fourteen days. (The soil round the plants must be kept moist before applying any liquid feeds or compost mulches – as for all crops.) It is important to keep cauliflowers well watered.

Give a double handful of veganic compost round each plant when they are growing well, two to three weeks after planting, and a further two mulches during their growth.

Harvest cauliflowers when the head is quite white and firm; it is a good idea to break down an outer leaf or two over the heads as they are forming, to keep them white and prevent them turning yellow.

Varieties for Late Summer/Autumn Heading

All the Year Round can be sown in January–February under glass, and March–May outdoors in a seedbed, also in September – early October in a cold frame to overwinter. Snowball, Autumn Giant and Veitch's Autumn Giant are sown in May. Some of the Australian varieties are extremely good, and are sown in late April–mid-May. Try Barrier Reef and Brisbane, heading late October and November.

Winter Cauliflowers Heading in January–April

These used to be known as broccoli but are now classified as either winter or hardy cauliflowers. They may take about twelve months from seed sowing to the formation of the heads ready for cutting.

Seed is sown during April or May, just as for all the brassicas. Plant out in June or early July, only one row on one side of a garden bed, with 2 feet (60 cm) between plants in the row. (This means two rows to a bed if required.)

Give a liquid feed of compost water or diluted seaweed solution at planting and every fourteen days, at the same rate as for the earliest kind, a little under a pint (0.5 l) to each plant.

As with late summer/autumn heading varieties, it is essential to keep the plants well watered, and for these winter types give at least two mulches of veganic compost of one good handful to each plant, the first about four weeks after planting and the second during August or September.

The following varieties are recommended for the milder areas and not cold and exposed sites:

Snowhite: ready for use March–April

Angers No. 1. Superb Early White, which heads in January – February.

Angers No. 2. Westmarsh Early, which matures February – March

Extra Hardy Varieties

These should not be sown before mid-May. It may be best for those with rather exposed gardens or allotments to consider having the really hardy types such as English Winter – Reading Giant, which heads in April. English Winter – Late Queen heads in May. Northern Star is recommended too, heading up in late May. Walcheren Winter-Thanet, heads late April, and Sutton's Walcheren Winter-Burchington matures late April to early May.

Broccoli
Sprouting Broccoli

White and purple sprouting broccoli, like curly kale, can withstand cold winters, and are extremely useful vegetables because they bear their shoots in spring and early summer when the majority of winter vegetables are finished.

Sow the seeds in April or early May,

and transplant into permanent positions in June or July. Plant only one row each side of a garden bed and space them about 2 feet (60 cm) apart in the row; really firm the soil round the stem. Broccoli needs plenty of moisture during the growth period, although it will withstand very dry conditions surprisingly well. After a few weeks apply a generous double handful of veganic compost to each plant. Do this at least twice during growth, and liquid feed with diluted seaweed solution at intervals of between fourteen and twenty-one days.

Improved White Sprouting and Early Purple Sprouting are ready for use in March–April. The latter is a compact form. Late Purple Sprouting is very hardy and ready in April. Like all brassicas they benefit by being grown in association with dill and chamomile.

When picking, always take the terminal flower head first; this will encourage the lesser sideshoots to develop.

Green Sprouting broccoli, or calabrese, is a relative newcomer to Britain. It is sown and transplanted just like the white and purple types, but is ready for picking in late summer and autumn. Hybrid types mature in nine to ten weeks. The plants are not winter-hardy.

Kale (Curly)
This is one of the two greens which will grow quite well even in poorish soils. On an undug strip garden bed enriched with veganic compost it will produce an abundance of its curled leaves and during a very hard winter is one of the few brassicas to survive. Kales are not prone to pest or disease once past the seedling stage.

Sow seeds in the prepared seed bed as for other brassicas, in shallow drills with about 5 inches (13 cm) between the rows. Water the drills if the soil is dry. Sow in April, set out the plants in June

or early July in two rows on one side of a garden bed – the row nearest the path about 6 inches (15 cm) from the edge and the second row some 18 inches (45 cm) in from the first. Space the plants 2 feet (60 cm) apart in the rows. Compost water or liquid feed at planting time and every twenty-one days during the summer, at the rate of 1 pint (0.5 l) to each plant. Give a mulch of veganic compost on moist soil around each plant during the summer period, and keep up watering. The young leaves may be picked when the plant is about 15 inches (38 cm) tall.

Probably the best-known variety is Tall Green Curled, which is very hardy. Pentland Brig is one of the best to grow, only 16 inches (40 cm) to 18 inches (45 cm) tall and cropping from November to May. Another excellent variety is the Dwarf Green Curled, which is useful for those with exposed gardens.

As with all brassicas, keep the beds weeded, preferably by hand so as not to damage the fibrous roots. Make sure the weeds hidden behind the large leafy plants do not run into flower and seed. In other words remove weeds to the compost heap when young and before seeding.

Sweet Corn
Sweet corn, or corn on the cob, is really a cereal, but when boiled as a vegetable is delicious (see picture 19). A native of America, it now enjoys ever-increasing popularity both in Britain and on the Continent. It is a fairly straightforward crop to grow, providing it is protected from winds. It needs an open, sunny plot and a soil enriched with veganic compost and given liquid feeds through the summer.

Outdoor Sowing
Sweet corn can be sown in position

Picture 19 Sweet corn will happily grow if it is protected from winds and planted in a sunny spot.

outdoors in early May in the south and towards the end of May in the north. If the basic soil of the plot is in reasonable condition then it will probably take four rows per bed, otherwise only two.

The four rows should be 12 inches (30 cm) apart, with the first row 9 inches (23 cm) from the edge of the bed. At intervals of 14 inches (35 cm) in each row – and these can be staggered – make holes by removing soil to a depth of approximately 2½ to 3 inches (6 cm to 7.5 cm) and put into each hole a small handful of veganic compost. On this compost place two sweet corn seeds 2 inches (5 cm) apart, cover with 1½ inches (4 cm) of soil and firm with the back of the hand. Keep the seeds moist and when the seedlings are well formed remove one from each station, leaving the stronger one to grow on. Be careful not to disturb the roots of the one retained. Simply pinch off at the base of the seedling to be removed. Sweet corn dislikes root disturbance; any weeds close to the seedlings should be removed by hand; scrap-weed only between the mature plants.

When the young plants are about 6 inches (15 cm) high, apply a liquid feed of either veganic compost water or diluted seaweed solution, at the rate of 1 pint (0.5 l) to each young plant. One capful or 6 teaspoonfuls (30 ml) of the concentrate seaweed solution to 11 pints (6 l) of water will be about right for 24 plants. Continue giving the liquid feeds at fourteen or twenty-one day intervals, but apply a pint (½ l) to each plant.

Keep up watering in dry weather and give a good double-handful mulch of veganic compost to each plant when 18 inches (45 cm) to 2 feet (60 cm) high, making sure the soil is moist before applying the compost.

Sweet corn will not bear unless pollinated. Male flowers appear at the top of the plants, usually 4½ to 5 feet (1.5 m) high, and the female flowers, which bear the cobs, form lower down the stem, their silky tassels catching the pollen which falls from the male flowers. This is why sweet corn plants need to be fairly close to one another to assist in pollination, since male and female flowers do not always emerge together. Even two rows on a garden bed with the rows about 22 to 24 inches (65 to 70 cm) apart with plants opposite one another and planted 14 inches (35 cm) in the row, will still pollinate and produce cobs. The stems may require staking to prevent wind damage. By early September the cobs should be ready, although this all depends on variety and the weather and it could be late September in the north.

Indoor Sowing

It may be as well to give sweet corn an early start by sowing one seed in a pot filled with veganic seed-sowing compost during mid-April to mid-May, especially for northern gardens. Keep the pots in a cold frame or cool greenhouse until ready for planting out of doors in late May or early June.

Prepare the garden bed in the manner already described for outdoor sowing and make each planting hole that bit larger to take the young sweet corn plant plus a good handful of compost to each hole.

Varieties

For sowing outdoors in the south the variety First of All is an excellent early one; often this matures by the end of August. Another reliable one is Kelvedon Glory (an F_1 hybrid), which with a good summer matures by early September. Those in the north should try First of All and Northern Belle.

Swedes

The swede is a frost-hardy, yellow fleshed root vegetable, though it is in fact one of the brassica family. The red soil of Devon produces particularly fine crops but with a little attention the average gardener can also produce delicious swedes by the surface cultivation (no digging) method and veganic compost routine.

In the north, seed can be sown about mid-May, and in the south, early June. Mark two rows using the back of the rake on one side of a garden bed, 18 inches (45 cm) apart, the first running 7 inches (18 cm) in from the edge, making a depression ¾ inch (2 cm) deep. The germination rate is normally very high, so the seed should be sown thinly, say two to the inch (2.5 cm). The second day after sowing, unless it has rained, water the ground with a fine mist spray, and during growth keep the bed watered at intervals using the surface method, especially in dry periods. When the seedlings are about 1½ inches (4 cm) high, thin out to 7½ inch (19 cm) spacings, leaving the most sturdy and vigorous seedlings. Swedes, in common with many brassicas, do occasionally grow blind, that is, with-

out a true growing centre, and such seedlings must be pulled out. It is better to retain healthy, sound seedlings even if the spacings in the row are not precise. The second and final thinning is to 15 inches (38 cm). After thinning, spread a good double handful of veganic compost with a little old domestic soot mixed in, around each root, pulling out any weed growth first. This spacing will provide medium-sized roots, which can be lifted as required throughout the winter period, or else they can all be lifted in October and stored under cover in dry sand.

Purple Top is a good reliable variety, especially for the north. There is also Sutton's Western Perfection, a quick-growing variety and often ready for lifting, as required, from September onwards.

Potatoes

Growing potatoes the veganic way ensures a clean and healthy crop, with a delicious flavour. Anyone with a small garden often likes the idea of growing a few earlies as well as some peas, since there is nothing quite like new potatoes with fresh garden peas to please the family.

Those with a larger garden or an average-sized allotment may well be able to grow early and maincrop varieties. Whatever is decided it is generally agreed that potatoes are fairly simple to look after. When grown in this newer way – no digging and veganic composting – they are exceptionally clean when lifted from the ground, a fact much appreciated by anyone preparing them for cooking.

When laying out the garden or the allotment for vegetables and soft fruit, it is best to set aside a permanent part of the plot for growing potatoes, as the soil will not transform itself when these are grown, mainly because planting disturbs the soil more than other crops. Therefore set aside a strip bed or beds for growing potatoes, plus the larger leafy crops such as brassicas or celery, which also require considerable soil disturbance at planting, and may be rotated with them. The potatoes, and anything else grown on the same beds, will need the same amount of compost each season, unlike the other crops, which require less compost after the first year.

When buying the seed potatoes examine them carefully, discarding any faulty or 'dud' specimens. Only retain those which are clean and perfect. Reputable firms normally supply tubers in a reasonably uniform size, and if possible select virus-free, certified stock from a garden centre, horticultural shop or farmer's merchant.

It is customary, though not vital, to sprout the tubers before planting and this will increase the yield as this gives them a longer time to mature before lifting them in the autumn. To sprout the tubers place them in a shallow tray or seed box in a good light with the 'rose' uppermost on each tuber – recognizable because it has a quantity of 'eyes' (tiny buds) fairly close together, which eventually grow to make the tops of the plant. Do this about six weeks before planting out.

Planting

Early Varieties
The suggested planting time is April, earlier in favoured areas – if frost threatens then strew clean straw over the young tops – thin cover only. The method of planting is the same whether the tubers have been pre-sprouted or not. Make sure the area is free of weed growth, by following the routine described for scrap-weeding. Then put two marking lines in position, one each side of the garden bed and about 14 inches (35 cm) in from the edge, then take the long hoe and walk sideways down the path from left to right, pulling the hoe through the soil, and drawing out a drill 6 inches (15 cm) deep.

Next place a really generous double handful of compost (one-third peat and two-thirds veganic compost) at estimated 12 inch (30 cm) intervals along the furrow. After applying the compost mixture, take the marking cane along the garden bed to check the distance between the compost 'mounds' in the furrow, and place a potato in each mound with the little sprouts upwards – it is best to remove all but two or three strong sprouts on each eye end. To complete the planting remove the marking lines and cane and with the long hoe cover the potatoes carefully with soil. Thus where the drills were, there will now be two rows of slight mounds along the garden bed or beds until the tops of the potatoes are 3 to 4 inches (7.5 to 10 cm) high. Then pull the weeds by hand into a container for composting. As the surface soil is cleared in this way, draw up more soil around the potato mounds about 2 inches (5 cm) up the growing tops.

Planting in furrows allows the concentration of plant foods from the compost to be readily available and allows the potatoes to be earthed up as the foliage grows.

No other attention apart from watering occasionally should be necesssary. Further weed growth is allowed to grow alongside until the crop is lifted, which is usually as it is required for the table.

Maincrop
Plant from April onwards. The first fortnight in May is not too late for a worthwhile crop. Follow the same

routine as for the earlies except that the tubers need to be planted 15 inches (38 cm) between each other.

Maincrop plants usually die down in September. Lifting is facilitated if the haulms can be cut off first. Choose a dry day for lifting and use a fork. On a fine dry day the tubers can be left on the soil for a few hours or else placed on a sack in the sun to dry off, and then stored. However, it is best to examine them first, discarding any damaged ones. They can be stored on the floor of a cool, dark shed, but put down sacking or clean straw first. Cover with clean straw or clean sacking to exclude light and prevent greening.

Recommended varieties are:

First early: Arran Pilot; Duke of York; Pentland Beauty, Sutton's Foremost.

Second early: Pentland Dell; Catriona; Craig's Royal.

Maincrop: Arran Banner; King Edward; Maris Piper; Desiree.

Finally, do consider carefully if it is really worth growing a maincrop, as generally the early varieties are more palatable and therefore preferable if there is space available.

CHAPTER 10

HERBS

There is an ever-increasing interest in the many different kinds of herbs, whether for culinary, medicinal, aromatic or ornamental purposes. Most herbs play an important role within the garden itself, creating a healthy atmosphere, helping to protect against pests, and even helping to check disease in soils and plants.

When herbs become too big and unmanageable and need trimming, then such trimmings are extremely useful for compost making.

Every garden would benefit by the inclusion of these most useful and attractive plants.

In the main they are not too fussy about the type of soil they grow in. Strange though it may seem, some thrive in quite poor soil, but a sandy loam is best for the widest range of herbs, although angelica, parsley and mints will tolerate clay. The addition of veganic compost to heavy clay soil will render it more amenable and so ensure the growing of a wider range of herbs.

The most commonly used culinary herbs can easily be accommodated in a small home garden or allotment, if it has a sunny spot. Parsley, mint and chives can even be fitted in where there is only semi-permanent shade. Herbs will fit happily into tubs or containers or in soil squares in a patio or paved area, and require little attention other than regular watering in dry spells.

Whether annual, herbaceous peren-nial or evergreen, many herbs would fit into a flower garden or mixed border and be a great asset with access to them, if borders are wider than 3 feet (90 cm), by stepping onto flattish stones or bricks.

If larger quantities are needed it is better to grow them in the vegetable section or even use them to edge a border, particularly those treated as annuals.

If your garden has sufficient herbs for culinary and medical purposes then why not put aside an area where herbs alone grow round a seat, providing many different leaf colours and shapes, filling the air with evocative scents?

Herb Types
Annuals
These include basil, dill and borage. They are grown from seed and flower within twelve months of seeds bring sown. They die down completely. Should leaves be required for winter from the annuals then they will need to be dried.

Biennials
These include caraway and parsley. They flower during the second summer after sowing, and then die. They are hardy enough to survive and live through the first winter, when fresh leaves can be picked from them in southern areas. (Parsley, though a biennial, is generally grown as an annual.)

Perennials

These include lemon balm, mint, lovage, chives, bay, sage and thyme. Quite a number of perennials die down in the autumn and regrow again in the following year; these are the herbaceous perennials, and include mints, lovage and lemon balm.

Other perennials are woody and either lose their leaves in the autumn or are evergreen and their leaves may be gathered at any time of the year. Perennials, whether they are herbaceous or woody, are normally grown from small plants, formed from stem cuttings, division of plants or by layering, or grown from seeds.

Outdoor Sowing

The soil preparation for herb seed sowing is the same as described in Chapter 5, under 'Seed Sowing and Planting'. Sow the seeds thinly where they are to grow in rows on a garden bed or in patches in the flower border and cover them with ¼ inch (6 mm) of soil. Water in with a fine spray. It is essential to protect the seeds and seedlings from birds.

Planting

Young plants are usually available in containers at most garden centres and garden shops, or from the increasing number of herb nurseries. The best times for planting out container-grown plants are spring or autumn, but any time is acceptable provided the weather is not too cold or wet.

Before planting, make sure the soil is moist, and be careful not to break up the soil ball, as it is knocked out of the container. With the planting knife or trowel make a hole big enough to accommodate both the soil and a handful of veganic compost for each plant.

Plant so that the surface of the soil ball is just below the level of the bed soil. Fill in with soil, firm well and water in.

If the soil is very stony or sandy, then apply a mulch of mature veganic compost to each plant in late spring or early summer.

During growth, the plant must be kept free of weeds. It is better to hand-pull these rather than attempting to use the scrapper in case the roots are damaged. Generally, watering is hardly ever needed, except for newly planted stock or seedlings.

The section below, to the end of this chapter, lists a selection of useful herbs and describes their cultivation.

Parsley   (*Petroselinum crispum*)

Although this is a hardy biennial, it is usually grown as an annual. If sown one year to use the next, then it will normally remain fresh in the garden for two years from sowing, providing it is picked often enough and the centre of the plant is left. Never allow parsley to flower. If it does run into flower, just cut it back to 6 inches (15 cm) above the base and new shoots will emerge. Sow thinly in a part-shaded area in moist soil, in ½ to ¾ inch (12 to 18 mm)) deep drills. Sprinkle some old soot in the drills at the time of sowing.

Germination is slow – and it could take as long as seven weeks. Thin out when seedlings are an inch (2.5 cm) high or so, spacing them out to 9 inches (23 cm) apart in the row.

In dry weather keep the soil moist, and after the plants have been thinned out give them an occasional feed of liquid seaweed solution.

A good curled variety is Champion Moss Curled, although Paramount is said to be the hardiest. French or plain-leaved varieties have become more widely available in recent years and some maintain they have a superior flavour. Time to sow is from April onwards, and a further sowing can be made in June and August. Keep free of weeds.

Parsley is a good plant to have in borders or on a strip garden bed interplanted with onions and certainly with tomato plants.

Chives (Allium schoenoprasum)
This is a hardy bulbous perennial and is one of the easiest herbs to grow. Chives can be raised by sowing seeds outdoors in the spring, and can be increased by division. (They are also available in small pots from garden centres.) Sow the seed thinly in April to June. They need to be sown or planted in a sunny part of the garden or allotment. Chives are also propagated by dividing their roots, gently easing the small groups of tiny onions apart, and replacing them 6 to 9 inches (15 to 23 cm) apart. Plant 1 inch (2.5 cm) deep.

The plants will continue to increase each year and can then be divided in alternate years. To keep the plants in a healthy condition, apply a thin covering of compost during the summer.

Chives are valuable in warding off pests as well as fungal diseases

Thyme (Thymus spp.)
The common Thyme (Thymus vulgaris) is a shrubby perennial with a rich pungent scent, and grows to about 12 inches (30 cm) high.

The other culinary type is the lemon thyme, which is smaller, growing to 10 inches (28 cm) in height, and combines the thyme and lemon flavour.

Common thyme plants may be raised from seed sown in spring in pots or boxes, and then moved to large pots to be planted out the following spring, with the soil ball intact. Sow in April or May.

Lemon thyme is sterile and must be propagated by cuttings. Propagation is usually by cuttings removed with a 'heel' and rooted in a sandy compost.

Garden centres have them available in small pots and this is the easiest way to get them established in the garden. Plant in a sunny spot. No particular care is required except to cut back the plants after flowering to encourage new growth.

There are many other varieties of thyme, some of which (caraway, creeping lemon, wild) have some culinary and medicinal qualities. Specialist herb books and herb nursery catalogues will help in choosing from the purely decorative type.

Rosemary (Rosmarinus officinalis)
A very easy herb to grow, it is more or less a hardy evergreen, and ornamental. Though a native of the Mediterranean region it will survive the cooler temperate climes, except in severe winters

Young plants can be obtained from garden centres and shops. They need to be planted in a sunny, well-drained part of the garden in April or May.

One plant ought to be sufficient for a garden, and it can even be planted at the base of a south-facing wall and trained onto it.

Propagation is from cuttings taken with a 'heel' in summer and rooted in pots containing soil and sand.

It is important to get a hardy kind, which can be either blue or white-flowered, first, as some, including the pink-flowered variety, are only half hardy. There are upright and prostrate types.

Mint (Mentha spp.)
The many types of mint are all perennial, flowering mostly in mid to late summer and vary in height from 9 inches (23 cm) to about 4 feet (1.22 m). They prefer a partially shaded and

moist site, but tolerate a wide variety of positions.

Most mints are invasive and need attention annually or containing in some way. Inserting slates down into the soil to form a square or oblong shape, or using bricks at least three deep round the proposed area, will give an effective barrier for some months, but the searching underground stems will find the gaps and force their way through in a year or two. If you want to have the mints in one area for sometime, then one or more very large earthenware pots sunk into the ground to leave 2 inches (5 cm) proud of the soil level will effectively contain them.

Alternatively, they can be grown in tubs and set out on the patio or paved area, but attention to watering is necessary. To be sure of having a good-flavoured culinary or correctly named mint it is best to buy plants from a reliable garden centre or herb nursery. Mints hybridize very early and so only seed from the most trustworthy source can be sure to be as described.

Seed may be sown in March to April outdoors in drills ½ inch (12 mm) deep. Once established they are extremely easy to propagate, by dividing the roots in the spring and laying 6 to 9 inch (15 cm to 23 cm) lengths in very shallow drills and covering with about 2 inches (5 cm) of soil. It is advisable to have a fresh site every three years, or the soil in the containers can be changed. This is because mints tend to deplete soils unless adequately enriched with humus. If their rambling, rampant nature can be accepted they can be planted in flower beds, or borders to create a ground cover effect, especially in combination, e.g. the lower variegated ginger mint with the dark peppermint one.

Culinary mints
Apple Mint (*M. suaveolens*, syn. *M. rotundifolia*) 2 feet (60 cm).

Bowles Mint or Tall Apple Mint (*M. × Villosa nm. alopecuroides*). This mint is sometimes confused with apple mint, but is far more vigorous, reaching 4 feet (1.22 m) high, with leaves 2 to 3 inches (5 to 7.5 cm) long. It is occasionally sold as apple mint, or described as *M. rotundifolia* 'Bowles variety'.

Raripila Mint (*M. raripila rubra*).

Herb teas
Peppermint (*M. × piperita*).

Decorative mints
Ginger Mint (*M. × gentilis variegata*). Sometimes called pineapple mint, it has smooth green and yellow leaves. Low growing.

Variegated Apple Mint (*M. suaveolens variegata*). Also sometimes called pineapple mint, it has hairy cream or white and green leaves. The least invasive mint, it does not need to be restricted by slates or a sunken container.

For the herb lawn
Pennyroyal (*M. pulegium*). The creeping form.

Amongst paving stones
Corsican Mint (*M. requienii*). The smallest mint, up to ½ inch (12 mm) high with very tiny flowers.

Pond edges
Water Mint. (*M. aquativa*). The mint the Romans used.

Lemon Balm   *(Melissa officinalis)*
This is a hardy herbaceous perennial which dies down in the autumn. It grows to a height of 2 feet (60 cm) and is easily grown in any type of soil. Sow seeds outdoors in April and thin out in stages to 2 feet (60 cm) apart. Cut the foliage back to 6 inches (15 cm) above ground level in June to encourage more young shoots. In October, cut all the growth back to just above ground level. Lemon balm thrives in the garden and is an excellent plant for bees.

Basil   *(Ocimum spp.)*
Basils are the half-hardy annuals of branching upright habit. Do not sow outdoors before June in the south of England. In the north, outdoor sowings are inadvisable except in very warm sheltered spots. Indoor sowings in late April, should not be planted out until June. The characteristic clove-like scent is found unacceptable by some, but the herb is popular in salads and pasta dishes and is the perfect complement to tomatoes in any form.

Sweet Basil   *(Ocimum basilicum)*. This is the commonest type and is particularly suitable for outside growing, along with the lettuce-leaved basil and the dark opal form with its purple leaves and pink flowers. For container and pot growing, bush basil *(Ocimum minimum)* is a better choice with its more compact habit and small leaves. The smallest is Greek basil with tiny leaves, which can be snipped straight into salads with the kitchen scissors.

Basil is a useful plant in the vicinity of cucumber and courgettes and is a help in keeping them healthy.

Dill   *(Anethum graveolens)*
A useful, hardy annual, growing to about 3 feet (90 cm) with bluish-green thread-like leaflets and flat clusters of tiny yellow flowers. Needs a well-drained sunny site. Sow continuously April–June in drills ½ inch (12 mm) deep and 9 inches (23 cm) apart.

Dill being an annual is particularly suitable for sowing near carrots as they are mutually beneficial. It is also a valuable plant with all the brassica family as well as cucumbers.

Borage   *(Borage officinalis)*
A hardy annual which grows to about 3 feet (90 cm) but is variable in height, borage needs a sunny, sheltered position, but can manage in partial shade.

This is a herb that deserves to be in any flower border, and the brilliant blue flowers, although not scented, attract the pollinating insects, particularly bees. Borage is not too fussy about soil conditions, and seed can be sown where plants are to be in the garden. Sow in April or May and again in July to maintain supply. Thin out later.

After the first year it will reappear from the many seeds that survive the winter, although these are often not what you would have planned.

If in the vegetable section of a garden it is better to pick the leaves and not allow the plant to run into flower as it can become too dominant.

French Tarragon   *(Artemisia dranunculus)*
Tarragon is a perennial plant and the French tarragon is superior to the Russian, which is a lighter green with rough leaves not really worth growing. A sheltered position is important because a severe winter can kill tarragon. Although it really requires a well-drained open type of soil, a heavy one is suitable provided it is enriched with veganic compost some time before planting.

Garden centres supply plants in small containers and the best time for planting is in September, otherwise later March.

Tarragon can also be propagated by root division in the autumn, even from cuttings taken in July and rooted in a mixture of equal parts sand and loam compost. (The latter can be made by rotting down turf.) The plants are put out in the spring.

Chervil *(Anthriscus cerefolium)*
A hardy annual generally grown as an annual and flowering in summer, chervil is best raised from seed sown in a position in the sun. Start in early March, and make successional sowings through to September; it is essential to sow where the plants are to grow. Sow as thinly as possible and thin out when the seedlings are large enough to handle. Sow about ½ inch (12 mm) deep, and thin to 10 inches (25 cm) apart.

Remove the flowers just before they open and keep the soil round them moist.

The flavour is sweet and aromatic and the leaves are used to garnish, rather as parsley. Chervil is a useful plant for growing next to lettuces, and the pungent smell discourages ants.

Sage *(Salvia officinalis)*
This herb is virtually an evergreen shrub and flowers in midsummer. It will grow to a height of at least 2½ feet (76 cm) and spread even wider. Sage requires a well-drained soil and will respond to a mulching of veganic compost as it is shallow-rooting.

Plants may be obtained from a garden centre or shop, or seed may be sown in late April and the plants thinned out to 12 inches (30 cm) apart.

Propagation is by taking cuttings in July, preferably with a 'heel', and rooted in sandy loam compost. Trim over the plants after flowering to encourage

bushy growth, but do not cut so far down that shoots older than the current season's are pruned, otherwise new growth will be weak. It is best to replace every fourth year, as it can get rather straggly. A broad-leaf variety can sometimes be found at garden centres or herb nurseries, and it has the advantage of large leaves and virtual absence of flowering shoots.

A red-purple leaved sage is decorative, whilst having medicinal properties for sore throats. Golden sage and tricolour sage are both very decorative with variegated leaves, though the latter is tender.

Sage plants are useful for both home garden and allotment. A few can be planted down the centre of a strip garden bed and allowed to grow for two or three years. Sage is extremely beneficial for brassicas, which could well occupy the same garden bed.

Marjoram
There are three culinary marjorams:
1. *Origanum marjorana*, the sweet or knotted marjoram;
2. *Origanum onites*, the pot or French marjoram;
3. *Origanum vulgare*, the common marjoram or oregano.

Sweet marjoram is a half-hardy perennial normally grown as an annual by sowing outdoors in late April or early May in drills ½ inch (12 mm) deep by 6 to 10 inches (15 to 25 cm) in rows, apart and the seedlings thinned out at the 1 inch (2.5 cm) stage to 12 inches (30 cm) in the row. In the north, seed is better sown in a greenhouse, frame or on a sunny windowsill in pots. Plant out in May or June.

Pot marjoram and oregano gets up to 2 feet (60 cm) in some clones. They can also be sown from seed, but as both are hardy the sowings can be earlier, March or April, and will only be needed for the first year. Plants of all three types are generally available from garden centres or a herb nursery but be sure to choose the correct plant for your needs. Sweet marjoram is generally the herb referred to as 'marjoram' in recipes and has a slightly sweeter flavour than others. Some regard pot marjoram as the most pungent and the best to have, but there is quite widespread confusion between this and the common wild marjoram. To be absolutely sure which of these two you are getting it is best to go to a large herb nursery. The difference in flavour is only slight, however, and may be of more interest to the gourmet.

Oregano is a wild plant common to much of Europe, from the Mediterranean to Britain. It is therefore variable in growth and proportion depending on where the plant originally came from.

However, the plant bought from a garden centre or nursery has been selected for its culinary properties. Marjorams need plenty of sunlight; also make sure the garden bed has been well cleared of weeds and enriched with veganic compost, prior to sowing the seeds. (Refer to Chapter 5, under 'Seed Sowing and Planting'.) In the autumn cut the plant back hard and string into a bunch to dry in an airy room. Fresh seeds should be sown each year, although it is possible that plants will survive a mild winter.

Fennel *(Foeniculum vulgare)*
A hardy perennial with a thick taproot, it looks like a greener, taller dill, but at 4 to 5 feet (1.2 to 1.5 m) tall with a liquorice scent and flavour it is easily distinguished. Although perennial in many colder, wetter areas, it may act more as a biennial or annual. Find it an open sunny position if it is to be a specimen plant for which purpose the bronze-leaved form is particularly suit-

able. Both colours are very attractive in a herbaceous border. If a supply of leaves for salad or culinary flavouring is more important, broadcast seed or sow thinly in a shallow drill.

The fennel root itself can be used in salads or as a cooked vegetable.

Chamomile
This herb will be known to those who like herbal teas, but there are in fact three chamomiles. Common or Roman chamomile (*Chamaemelum nobile,* syn. *Anthemis nobilis* is a perennial with white single flowers and grows to 8 inches (20 cm). Wild or German chamomile (*Chamomilla recutita*) looks very much the same as Roman chamomile, but can grow up to 20 inches (50 cm) in a more erect form and is an annual.

The best variety to use for chamomile lawns is a hybrid of Roman chamomile, called 'Treneague'; the regular mowing of the lawn to eradicate the flowers is dispensed with because 'Treneague' does not produce any flowers, and is low and creeping in habit. Any initial costs, however, will be much greater as nine small plantlets are needed for each square foot (900 sq cm) of lawn.

The dried flowers of both annual and perennial types can be used for teas as they seem to have the same properties, although the annual plant is often referred to and most often used for medicinal purposes. It is said to have a soothing action on the digestive system and a sedative effect on the nervous system.

Sow in spring in rows 8 to 12 inches (20 to 30 cm) apart, thinning out only if the seed was sown rather too thickly – which is easy to do with fine seed.

The annual chamomile will self-sow readily if a few flowers are left to go to seed each year.

Bay *(Laurus nobilis)*

The bay (sweet laurel) is an evergreen tree-like shrub and a native of southern Europe, and yet it will stand being planted outdoors in England, provided it is planted in a sunny, fairly sheltered position and in a relatively mild area. Alternatively, it can be in a tub and brought indoors in the winter months.

It can look very interesting if formally clipped into either a pyramid, square or round head on a stem of about 3 to 4 feet (1 m) long; out of doors it can grow to 10 feet (3 m) or more and form a thickish hedge, or be kept on a clear stem to 5 to 6 feet (1.5 to 1.83 m) and the top grown and trimmed to a parasol shape.

For Planting Outdoors

It will grow in most types of soil, providing it is given a fairly sheltered site which receives a lot of sun. Preferably plant outdoors only in the south of England, as it is somewhat subject to frost damage in a very severe winter.

Bay can be grown on a single stem, and any suckers ought to be removed unless a hedge is required. They are very slow growing, require very little pruning, just a light clipping in the spring to maintain shape. If they can be protected in\the winter they will stay evergreen. Bays are propagated from cuttings of the new season's wood, removed in July, and preferably with a 'heel' attached. These cuttings are then inserted into a sandy compost and kept moist.

For Planting in a Tub

This will need to be a minimum diameter of 2 feet (60 cm). It is essential to provide ample drainage. Mix up soil, sharp gritty sand and veganic compost (two parts soil, and one part compost including the sand). Keep the mixture in the tub moist in dry weather and give a light mulch of compost each spring.

Lavender *(Lavandula spp.)*

Like the bay it is a native of southern Europe and classed as a shrubby perennial. Lavender is useful for its oils as well as being formed into low hedges. There are a number of varieties which survive the winter. They flower during July and August, and are aromatic. Most dwarf and semi-dwarf lavenders grow up to 2 feet (60 cm) in height and the standard ones well over 2 feet (60 cm).

Planting

In spring or autumn (October is best) take cuttings with a 'heel' and root outdoors in a sheltered place. Alternatively, buy small plants in containers from a garden centre. For growing lavenders as hedges plant 1 to 1½ feet (30 to 45 cm) apart in the row, and for a taller hedge plant 2½ feet (75 cm) apart choosing, of course, the standard varieties.

After flowering trim the bushes, but avoid cutting into the old wood. Lavender hedges do tend to become rather bare at the base unless trimmed in the spring.

Species cultivated

L. spica (syn. *L. officinalis*), the common lavender, grows to 4 feet (1.2 m) with purple flowers in mid-to-late summer.

L. vera (syn. *L. spica vera*), Dutch lavender, grows 2 feet (60 cm) with a dense habit and wide silver leaves, bearing pale-blue flowers on long spikes in July to August.

Named cultivars

The following are garden varieties of the species:

L. spica 'Folgate' is a good variety for low hedges, with lavender-blue flowers.

L. spica 'Hidcote' makes a good hedge of deep purple blue, 1 to 1½ feet (30 to 45 cm).

L. spica 'Nana Munstead Dwarf' is compact, with lavender-blue flowers, and grows to 1 foot (30 cm) high.

L. spica 'Grappenhall' variety is a strong grower up to 3 feet (90 cm) with broader and greener leaves.

L. spica 'Twinkle Purple' grows to 2 to 3 feet (60 to 90 cm) with bright purple flower spikes.

For hedging set the plants 12 inches (30 cm) apart, depending on the eventual height of the one chosen.

CHAPTER 11

GROWING FRUIT

More and more families are interested in growing some kind of fruit in their own gardens, whether it is simply a few strawberries or some raspberries or blackcurrants. Also, the prospect of planting an apple or pear is especially appealing now that fruit can be gathered without ladders and, thanks mainly to the many rootstocks available today, fruit can be picked from a three-year-old apple tree.

Since the early 1950s new varieties of cane and bush fruit have been introduced which now make it possible to gather and enjoy these fruits over a longer period. There are now frost-resistant and late-flowering raspberries which together with mid-season varieties can provide a succession of fruit from July to late autumn. There are now frost-resistant varieties of strawberries which can be grown where late frosts occur.

Most garden centres and fruit tree nurseries supply a wide range of both trees and soft fruit, and if you follow the directions given here you should be able to grow any fruit in an easy and straightforward way, particularly in view of the no-digging technique.

Try to prepare the ground that is destined to be planted by clearing it in the manner described in Chapter 3. If possible, this should be done well before planting, the best time for which is the autumn or early winter period.

All trees and soft fruits benefit from mulches of compost – and this can be semi-mature – as well as the addition of bonfire ash or wood ash. Spread the ash in a dry state, sprinkling it at the rate of a handful to the square yard (0.83 sq.m.) in a circle as far as branches extend. Granite dust, sometimes sold as a fine silver sand, is very useful as it helps to increase flavour, but supplies tend to be limited to certain areas of the country.

It is best to keep all cane and bush fruit away from trees. And do keep up with the pruning and feeding.

Strawberries

Strawberries are a relatively straightforward crop to grow and maintain, providing a few simple rules are adhered to. They dislike cold winds, and although they are of woodland origin the modern strawberry requires plenty of sun, so select an open sunny part of the garden or allotment.

With so many varieties being available it is easy to extend the season from June (early varieties) through to July (maincrop) to September. It is essential to thoroughly prepare the soil of the garden bed, removing all weeds well in advance of planting time. They appreciate a humus-filled soil in good structure rather than extra compost being applied during their growth though additional mixture of compost and peat will be beneficial. It is better to buy in 'maiden' plants which are from certified stock –

the grower having received a Ministry of Agriculture 'A' certificate guaranteeing that the plants are free from virus and Red Core. ('Maidens' are taken from 1-year-old plants and are the most vigorous.) Buy pot-grown plants rather than open-ground runners, particularly for planting in July or August for fruiting the following June. The same applies to late July or August plantings for the main fruiting season of July.

Open-ground runners can be planted in October or November for fruiting the following late summer or autumn. With these late-summer and autumn-fruiting varieties, it is best to pinch off the first cluster of flowers – usually produced in the following May or June – to ensure a good crop of berries later on. As a rule, strawberries yield well for the first three years, but then they should be discarded.

Planting
Use a planting trowel and make holes large enough to take the roots and a good handful of compost for each plant. This applies whether the soil has been composted or not. Spread the roots out and see that the crown of the plant (the thick part) is just at soil level, and firm the plant in with your fingers. Give plenty of water if soil is dry, as strawberries need moist conditions.

Aftercare and Maintenance
As strawberries are surface-rooting, care will need to be taken when removing weeds. Moist ground will make the job easier. Hand pull the weeds and be careful not to damage the surface roots, when using the scrapper. When they begin to form their flowering trusses then apply a mulch of veganic compost and peat – half and half – to help conserve moisture and to feed the surface roots. They greatly benefit by the application of liquid feeds of either

compost water or diluted seaweed solution every ten days at the rate of 6 litres to every six plants, from flowering time until picking.

If planting on one side of a garden bed have two rows staggered, 16 inches (40 cm) between the rows and 18 inches (45 cm) in the row, the first row to be 8 inches (20 cm) in from the bed edge.

During the first year, pinch off all the runners from the parent plant. If you do not wish to start another bed then pinch off the runners during the second season as well.

In the second or third year allow one or two runners to form on each parent plant, peg these into the soil and when they are rooted, which will be in a few weeks, sever from the main plant. These runners are then planted out in a new bed for fruiting the following year.

To keep the berries clean push a little new straw underneath each fruit cluster. Only do this when the fruit has started to form, not whilst it is in flower.

Protection from birds is essential and this can be provided by supporting netting 8 inches (20 cm) or so above the plants on canes.

Varieties
For fruiting in June the following are recommended:

Red Gauntlet. A heavy cropper but only fair in flavour.

Cambridge Vigour. Medium-sized fruit of good flavour.

Grandee. A continental variety with large bright-red berries of good flavour. This variety produces a large crop of fruit in the second season.

Pantagruella, like Grandee, produces berries of a good size and flavour.

Royal Sovereign has the best flavour of all strawberries, but is somewhat prone to virus infection; the flower stalks tend to be rather on the long side and thus liable to suffer from frost damage.

Koroma, Maxim and Tamella are the new Dutch varieties worth trying, especially the last-named.

Late July to October-fruiting varieties:

Gento has fruit of good flavour and crops well.

Bogota, Domanii and Tentra are good Continental varieties which ripen in August and early September.

Domanii yields a heavy crop of large wedge-shaped dark red berries.

Hampshire Maid is another fine autumn-fruiting variety, a good cropper with bright red fruit.

Alpine Strawberries

These bear small but delicately flavoured berries towards the end of the summer period. They do not form runners and are easy to look after.

Possibly the best place to plant them is at the edges of stone or brick paths rather than letting them take up space on garden beds. Plants are available from garden centres or can be raised from seed by sowing outdoors in April.

Alpines generally fruit in late June, followed by another batch in July and August. It is best to discard the plants after two seasons. The variety Baron Solemacher is a popular one, compact and bushy in form with light green foliage. The fruit is best picked when fully ripe.

Blackcurrants

It is always well worthwhile to grow a bush or two of this most popular fruit, known for its high vitamin C content. Blackcurrants grow best in an open, sunny position in soil well enriched with vegetable compost and sheltered from cold winds. They are more frost-tender than most fruits. They are self-fertile.

Soil Preparation and Planting

It pays to prepare the soil well before planting, and if new planting is planned the initial soil preparation is important as the bushes will continue to crop for at least twelve years.

If possible, spread a bucketful of veganic compost at every 6 feet (1.83 m) in the centre of a bed 4 feet or 4 feet 6 inches (1.22 or 1.37 m) wide, on clear soil at least two months before planting out 2-year-old bushes. Remove the soil with a fork, making holes a little larger than the root span, and set the bushes at a depth 2 inches (5 cm) greater than the soil mark left by their time at the nursery, so that the branches appear to emerge from the soil. After planting, cut these branches off to within an inch (2.5 cm) of soil level. This drastic measure ensures ample new growths from the base, which is always the aim with pruning blackcurrants. Planting can be done from October through to February, so long as the soil is reasonable in texture, and not too wet and sticky.

After planting apply a mulch of compost (this can be only semi-mature) at about a gallon to each plant.

Always be sure to buy certified stock from a good source.

Maintenance and Pruning

In April each year mulch each bush with a gallon or more of compost which can be semi-mature and from mid-May to September liquid feed every fourteen days with a gallon of either compost water or seaweed solution. See also that the bushes receive adequate amounts of water as blackcurrants require copious amounts; never allow the soil around them to dry out.

The spring mulch with compost is particularly important because this encourages the formation of new wood, which bears the best-quality and largest berries. As regards pruning, the shoots made in the first year after planting are left untouched at the end of the season. These will bear some fruit the next summer, but at the end of that year two or three of the shoots should be cut down to two or three buds.

The basic aim of pruning established blackcurrants is to cut up to a third of the old shoots which have produced fruit, and leave as much young wood as possible. Cutting down the old shoots to soil level encourages new growth from below the soil. When selecting old shoots for removal, aim to alleviate crowding and to remove cross branches in particular.

There should never be any branches older than 4 years.

Blackcurrants, along with other soft fruits, are surface-rooting, and extra care needs to be taken when weeding so that the fibrous root system is retained undamaged.

Early Varieties
Boskoop Giant. An early and fairly heavy cropper; growth large and spreading. Better in a warm, sheltered garden.

Laxton's Giant. A really fine dessert – the first and only one – with very large, sweet and juicy fruit. A vigorous spreading bush with good resistance to disease and frost. Easy to pick.

Mendip Cross. One of the best earlies for a cold area. It is tolerant of frosts and cold winds and bears a heavy crop of medium-sized juicy fruits.

Wellington XXX. Makes a large spreading bush. A good all-round variety, and does well in most types of soil. Certainly one to have in a home garden.

Mid-season Varieties
Blacksmith. Does well in light soils, blooms late and is frostproof. Produces a heavy crop of berries. Also large and spreading in growth.

Seabrook's Black. A more compact, upright bush, ideal where space is limited. It blooms late and misses the frost. Ripens early and is resistant to big bud. Fruit a little on the acid side.

Late Varieties
Baldwin. The Hilltop strain is the best and only really crops well where soil and climate suit it. Does best in the south and prefers a light soil, but needs to be fed with compost mulches and given plenty of liquid feeds of either compost water or diluted seaweed solution to help it to grow new wood. A compact variety and could be planted at 5 feet (1.52 m) apart in the row.

Amos Black. A very late one and with compact upright habit, valuable for a small garden. It blooms late and escapes frost, and also ripens later than any. At its best in October, but fruit is a little on the acid side.

Jet. A fairly new one from East Malling Research Station in Kent. This too is late-flowering and late-ripening. It bears a particularly heavy crop on long stalks, so it is easy to pick.

There are a great many varieties and new ones keep appearing from research institutes both in the UK and in Holland. One from Scotland is Ben Lomond. This flowers late and so escapes frost damage. The berries are large with a good flavour.

Red and White Currants
Although not as popular as blackcurrants, these are nevertheless worthwhile growing as they stand drought conditions better than the blackcurrant.

Choose a sunny part of the garden, and plant 2-year-old bushes, as these are best. Also select a place in the garden which is sheltered from strong winds, which may break the rather brittle stems, as these bushes only make a small amount of wood. Soil preparation and planting are the same as for gooseberries, and the same planting period applies.

Both red and white currants fruit largely on two-year-old wood. The early stages of pruning are the same as for gooseberries and the actual pruning method adopted is as for dessert gooseberries, i.e. spur pruning. After planting, the bush should be allowed to settle in, the branches are then cut back to five or six buds from the base, and from the topmost buds growth will take place during the following season. The following winter, the strong shoots which form the framework of the bush are shortened to one half of their length.

All growth except the terminal shoot, which is the continuation of the branch, is pruned in the winter to two buds. At these points fruit will later be borne. Subsequent pruning is the same, always pruning back hard all the growth except branch extension.

Red and white currants benefit from a mulch of veganic compost, which may be semi-mature, in the spring around April to May at the rate of a gallon (4.5 l) per plant. Also, give them a regular feed of seaweed solution every fourteen days, at the same rate as for gooseberries. The white currant is merely a colour variation of the red, though with a finer flavour. At all times the soil must be moist when the compost is spread round the bushes.

Varieties of Red Currant
Jonkheer van Tets. An early currant and ready for picking at beginning of July.

Fruit of medium size, deep red, and flavour good. Fairly upright bush spurring freely, and a good cropper.

Laxton's No. 1. A mid-season variety, ready for picking about the middle of July. Medium-sized fruit, very bright red and juicy. Strong vigorous upright to spreading bush. Flowers late but crops well in all parts.

Red Lake. Probably the best red currant, it makes a large upright bush and bears heavy crops of very large berries. It withstands wet weather very well.

Varieties of White Currant
White Versailles. Early and ready for harvesting at the beginning of July. Has good-sized pale yellow fruits borne on strings of medium length. Strong upright bush.

Raspberries
These are some of the best fruits to have in a garden because it means that you can enjoy berries of a quality seldom available in a shop or market.

The raspberry is a hardy plant and the canes grow 4 or 5 feet (1.25 m) tall and bear heavily during July, August and September. The only drawback is that the raspberry fruits on new canes only, and so it will be eighteen months or so before a new planting fruits. Canes are normally planted during the late autumn and winter and then cut down to within 4 inches (10 cm) of soil level in the spring. The plants then send up new canes on which fruit is borne the following year. New canes form each season to take the place of those which have fruited and these latter are cut close to the ground. Raspberries will tolerate some shade, but select a part of the garden which enjoys at least half a day's full sun.

A 4 feet 6 inch (1.38 m) wide bed will take two rows 2 feet 6 inches (76

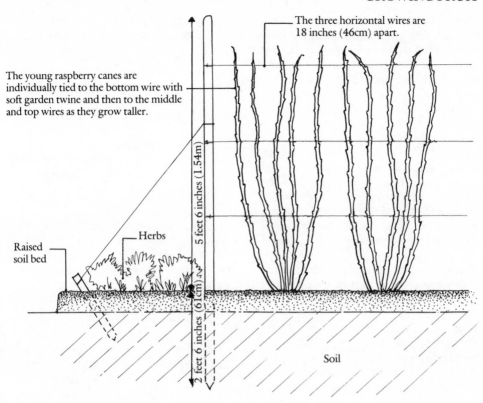

The three horizontal wires are
18 inches (46cm) apart.

The young raspberry canes are
individually tied to the bottom wire with
soft garden twine and then to the middle
and top wires as they grow taller.

Herbs

5 feet 6 inches (1.54m)

Raised
soil bed

2 feet 6 inches (61cm)

Soil

Picture 20 **Staking and training of raspberry canes.**
Posts are set in the ground and must be braced, either by wire (as shown here) or by using
diagonal supports.

cm) apart, with the plants 2 feet (60
cm) apart in the row, each row being
some 12 inches (30 cm) from the bed
edge. To support the canes it is essential
to have sturdy 6 foot 6 inch (2 m)
timber posts driven into the ground at
12 foot (3.7 m) intervals with three
strong wires stapled to them along the
rows, at 1½, 3 and 4½ feet (45 cm, 90
cm and 1.38 m) above ground level.
The end posts must be braced (see
picture 20).

Soil Preparation and Planting
It is essential to thoroughly clean and
prepare the soil for raspberry canes by

clearing weed growth and spreading
veganic compost on moist soil in two
bands (if there are to be two rows), each
12 inches (30 cm) wide (which will
mean the canes are planted in the centre
of each band). Endeavour to prepare
the soil about 4 weeks before planting.
It is important to obtain certified
virus-free stock from a specialist
nurseryman or a reliable garden centre.
  Autumn planting is advised, mainly
because soil conditions are usually
better than in December or January.
The best time is probably the last two
weeks in October to the first week in
November. Plant the canes with the

roots only just beneath the surface. Immediately after planting they should be cut back to within 4 inches (10 cm) of the soil level, or this can be left until the end of February. Keep the ground weeded by scrap-weeding, and take care not to damage the surface roots of the canes.

Give a mulch of compost in March or April, a gallon (4.5 l) round each plant, which can be semi-mature. In the summer and as new canes grow, fasten them to the wires using soft string. Keep the ground well watered, failing adequate rainfall, during any dry spell. The following spring, give a mulch of compost, a gallon (4.5 l) per plant. Endeavour to feed with diluted seaweed solution every fourteen days from April to July, at the rate of 1¾ pints (1 l) for two canes. The canes will need to be kept well watered throughout the spring and summer.

After fruiting, the 'old' canes are cut down to the ground and only the strongest four or five of the new canes retained per stool. This will mean that there is one cane for every 5 or 6 inches (13–15 cm) of wire. In particularly damp areas of the country this may prove to be too many as the fruit could suffer attacks of botrytis mould. In such areas, reduce the number of canes to two or three per stool. Remove any suckers which are growing any distance from the main rootstock – the raspberry is a 'roamer' if not kept in hand.

Early Varieties
Royal Scot. This is one of the best raspberries. It makes vigorous cane growth and is the first to mature in the north. The large berries are borne along the many branchlets. It is a most valuable kind for the home garden.

Malling Promise. Another early one and a rather vigorous grower, so it must be well controlled as it tends to produce many canes outside the actual row needed. A good one for southern areas.

Malling Jewel. A second early and one of the best all-round variety yet introduced, and is frost-hardy. A heavy cropper, and makes plenty of tall, smooth canes but needs a rich soil.

Mid-season Varieties
Glen Clova. Cane growth is vigorous and bears bright-red fruits. Suitable for northern areas as it blooms late and escapes frost.

Malling Notable. A little later than Jewel, it produces large fruit with good flavour. Has a short picking period as berries ripen almost all at once.

Malling Leo. One week later than Admiral. More resistant to virus. Large fruit but slow to establish, so double the planting rate.

Late Varieties
Malling Admiral. Grows large, firm dark-red berries in late July and August, and yields a consistently heavy crop irrespective of weather conditions.

Autumn-fruiting Varieties
These actually require the same culture as the others but fruit in the autumn on the new season's canes, which are cut back in late November after fruiting.

September. This variety fruits until well into October but is best grown in the south. A good one for a dryer, sandy soil.

Zeva. Originating in Switzerland, it is extremely hardy and fruit ripens from mid-August to end of October. The variety makes plenty of cane growth each year.

Gooseberries
The gooseberry is native to Britain where it has been cultivated since the

thirteenth century at least. As it is self-fertile and fairly productive by nature, it would seem an ideal soft fruit for a garden whatever the size. So even one bush in a small garden will yield a good crop.

Gooseberries are even hardier than blackcurrants and will tolerate most soils and respond to soils enriched with veganic compost. They thrive virtually anywhere in Britain, and do particularly well in the cooler climes of the north and midlands. Gooseberries really prefer full sun, but one or two varieties will grow in partial shade. It is most advisable to check with your local nurseryman who specializes in supplying soft fruit bushes, as he will be more likely to know which variety will thrive in your locality; some varieties definitely dislike certain soils.

All gooseberries must be thoroughly watered in dry spells, especially during the first year. Bonfire ash spread around the bushes is very beneficial, and they will need feeding with a generous mulch of veganic compost in April or May at the rate of half a gallon of compost per bush. From then onwards apply dilute seaweed solution every fourteen to twenty-one days, a litre per bush.

Planting
Gooseberries fruit on both old and new wood, so it is important for the plant to make good strong annual growth. Obtain 2 to 3 years old. Before planting remove buds and suckers below the main shoots. Also, remove any suckers which may be on the roots, but tear these off instead of cutting. Gooseberries are usually grown on a single leg or clear stem.

If you decide to have a bush type of plant then plant down the centre of a bed at 5 or 6 feet (1.52 m to 1.82 m) apart. They can be planted from early November until early March. With heavy soil a March planting is advised. Beds for gooseberries, blackcurrants and raspberries could be 4 feet (1.22 m) wide if desired. When planting spread out the roots and incorporate 2 gallons (9 l) of veganic compost per bush. The surface roots should be only just beneath the soil level when covered. During the first year many salad crops can be grown on the same bed as bush type gooseberries, using the space towards the edge of the bed.

Pruning of Bush Types
The early formative pruning is aimed at establishing a strong open framework. The first pruning consists of cutting back three or four strong shoots to an outward pointing bud leaving three or four buds from the base. This invariably means reducing the leaders by half to two-thirds their length. In the second year cut back 6 to 8 strong shoots (leaders) to half their length, to an outward-facing bud, and shorten the smaller sideshoots to one bud from the base. Once the bush is established, usually after the second year, then one needs to decide whether to use the regulated method or the spur method. The former consists in removing overcrowded, weak and old wood, and pruning branch leaders back by a quarter their length and 1-year-old shoots by 3 inches (7.5 cm). For spur pruning cut back all sideshoots to one or two buds to encourage the formation of fruiting spurs. This method will produce fewer but larger berries.

Cordons
Where space is limited it is a good idea to have a single or double cordon type. They can be planted alongside a path or against interwoven fencing tied in to strong wires. Single cordons can be planted 12 inches (30 cm) apart and set

at an oblique angle. A single cordon is trained by cutting back all the lateral shoots to a single bud. This forms the extension shoot which is grown on to a height of about 4 or 5 feet (1.22 or 1.52 cm). Then the new shoots formed in the summer are pinched back to within 2 inches (5 cm) of the base in late July or early August, after fruiting has finished.

Double cordons are slightly more difficult. Cut back the main stem (leader) to leave two buds about 8 or 9 inches (20 or 23 cm) from soil level. The buds should be on either side of the stem and from here new shoots are formed. Train the shoots which grow out from these buds at an angle of 45 degrees at first, held in place by two short canes fastened to the wires, later lowering them to horizontal. Tie these horizontal shoots on to wires, and then cut back to leave one upward-facing bud.

From the two buds, the shoots grow upwards parallel to each other and about 12 to 14 inches (30 to 35 cm) apart. After the first summer, they are then cut back to one bud about 6 inches (15 cm) above the horizontal formed shoots and from the bud the extension shoots. This forms the vertical framework of the cordon.

Use at least three wires along a row, the first some 12 inches (30 cm) above soil level.

Early Varieties
Keepsake. Dessert or cooking. A pale green oval of excellent flavour. A reliable cropper. This variety will need to have established shoots cut back to an upward bud to prevent drooping.

Whitesmith. A good strain of this variety will grow upright and vigorously and give a good crop of pale yellow fruit of excellent flavour for eating raw when ripe. Pick early for cooking.

Mid-season Varieties
Careless. Good for all purposes with berries almost oblong of whitish-yellow when ripe. It crops heavily in all types of soils.

Leveller. For dessert or cooking. With large fruit, smooth and yellow-green veins sharply marked. Good flavour and excellent cropper.

Lancashire Lad. The early fruit can be picked green for cooking and later, when it has ripened to deep red, for dessert. Bush is vigorous and spreading.

Whinham's Industry. Dessert or cooking, fruits large oval and sweet, ripening to dark red. An upright and vigorous growth later spreading. Does well in partial shade, and needs careful pruning for best results.

Late Varieties
Lancer (Howards Lancer). Dessert or cooking; fruit large, smooth. Vigorous growth and heavy cropper; and grows well on most soils.

White Lion. Dessert or cooking; fruits are white, large, and growth vigorous and erect. Good flavour.

Two new varieties have been introduced recently to make gooseberries even more worthwhile. The first is Invicta, which is very disease-resistant and produces heavy crop early in its life. Has large white or pale-green fruit which are easy to pick, being on longer than usual stalks. Another new variety is Captivator, which has red fruit and is entirely thornless.

It should be noted that varieties of spreading habit such as Keepsake and Whinham's Industry should have the established shoots cut back to an upward bud to counteract drooping habit. Those of upright habit need to be cut back to an outward pointing bud, to prevent the centre becoming overcrowded.

Apples

Providing the soil is fertile and the garden receives plenty of sun then growing apples should be no problem.

In any situation for apple growing, it is a good idea to have two compatible types of tree, a dessert and a cooker. When choosing, have two that are in flower at the same time so that cross-pollination is assured. There are varieties which can set a worthwhile crop entirely on their own, but the cropping of all varieties is improved with cross-pollination with another variety. Some kinds produce no proper pollen so cannot fertilize others. They are known as triploids. Selecting compatible cross-pollinators is an area in which next-door neighbours could well co-operate to mutual advantage.

For a small garden one can have a bush type, cordons, fan-trained trees or espaliers, and these should be on dwarfing or semi-dwarfing rootstock, depending on the type of soil. These types are relatively simple to manage when pruning and harvesting. There is usually a wide choice available at garden centres, and often these have been partly shaped by the nurseryman before delivery there. Normally, they are 2- or 3-year-old trees, and ideally should have four good main branches more or less at right angles to each other and at a fairly wide angle to the stem.

The trees will more than likely be in containers, which are convenient to carry away. On the other hand, trees sold with their roots bare can be inspected properly – look for a dense mass of fibrous roots and reject any with only a few thickish roots, or of course any with extensive damage.

A bush type will be less trouble to prune and maintain than cordons, which require posts and wires for support and need a little expertise to prune.

The choice of rootstock will depend in the main on the type of soil in the garden, whether it is fertile or just moderately so. A good indication is to observe how trees and shrubs are growing around the locality, and whether or not your garden soil has been under cultivation growing vegetables, flowers, etc., or indeed whether the only topsoil is that brought in when the house was built. Generally, a bush type of tree will flourish quite well in a small garden and is the most easily managed form of tree. It is advised that apples and pears are planted in one's own garden rather than on the allotment.

Listed below are the usual dwarfing and semi-dwarfing apple rootstocks suitable for the small to medium size garden with a brief description of each. For anyone with more space, wanting a larger tree, choose one with vigorous rootstock.

Dwarfing Stock

Malling 27. Growing to about 4 feet (1.2 m) in height and about half the size of those on Malling 9. Requires a fertile soil. If planting more than one bush tree on this rootstock then plant 12 feet (3.7 m) apart.

Malling 9. The most commonly used rootstock for dwarfing, needs a fertile soil, and will reach a height under average conditions of between 8 to 10 feet (2.4 to 3.0 m) and comes in bearing quickly. Plant between 12 and 15 feet (3.7 and 4.57 m) apart.

Semi-dwarfing Stock

Malling 26. Produces a tree larger and more sturdy than M9. Used for cordons and bush trees for small gardens. Needs a moderately fertile soil.

MM 106 (Malling Merton 106). An average quality soil will suit this rootstock. Has good anchorage on light land. It is an early cropper, and probably the best garden bush tree. Often used for cordon work.

Vigorous Stock

Malling 25 and Malling Merton 111. Although M25 is officially classified as more vigorous than MM 111, some nurserymen disagree. At any rate, half-standard or standard trees – the only kind which give headroom under them – probably need to be grown on one of these stocks if they are to stand in grass, that is on a lawn or in a paddock. Both rootstocks produce trees that bear fruit much sooner than the traditional crab stock.

If in doubt as to the right rootstock consult with your local expert at the garden centre or nurseryman specializing in fruit trees. Different varieties of apple make different sizes and shapes of trees on the same rootstock, a point always worth remembering.

Planting

The best time for planting is during November and December, providing the soil is neither frozen nor too wet to work freely. Make a hole large enough for all the roots to be spread out fully in their natural growing position. The subsoil should be thoroughly loosened with a fork, but not brought to the surface – this applies particularly to heavy soils. Fork in some sharp gritty sand if the soil is on the heavy side. See that the tree roots are moist, and remove wrapping or container, and trim off any minor root damage. Plant level with the soil on the stem, then carefully work in, on and around the roots, 2 gallons (9 l) of mature compost. (Before planting, set a vertical stout stake and plant the tree up against this support. Half-standard and stan-

dard trees require two stakes, each 12 inches (30 cm) either side of the tree, with a cross-piece just below the lowest branch.) Ensure the point of the graft union is at least 3 inches (7.5 cm) above soil level. Refill the hole with moist soil, and firm around the base. Water well.

Secure the tree to the stake or cross-piece with a protective tree tie to prevent wind damage. There are several types of tree 'ties', but the best is one which has a 'stopper' which comes between the tree and the stake and so prevents rubbing and possible damage. Use a broad-banded tie, not wire or string, as this kind of tie can be loosened as the stem thickens. Then surround the tree as far as the branches extend with a surface mulch of compost. During the early months the soil will settle and the tie will very likely need repositioning. You may also need to protect the tree from rabbits with a tree guard.

Planting in Grass

This is a term used when a tree is planted in the lawn, but in actual fact it is better for an apple tree to have a surround of bare soil for at least the first three years. Mark a circle or square 4 to 5 feet (1.2 m to 1.5 m) across, and with the spade remove 1 inch (2.5 cm) thick turves, from within the marked area, and stack them out of the way to become loam. Then follow the instructions already given. After planting and with the soil replaced spread 2 bucketfuls of veganic compost on the soil as far as the branches extend. Later, when the turves have become loam, return about half of it to the soil area around the tree. After three years you should decide whether to let the grass grow up to the tree. If it is cropping well it may be best to keep the ground bare. This also applies if the tree is not doing very well. On the other hand if it is well grown

Plate 5 (**a**) This is the best way to work under a Dutch light

(**b**) Cucumber plants growing in a cold frame

Plate **6** (*a*)   Natural stone sets off plants beautifully

(*b*)   Stone is used here to make a path

but producing little or no fruit then a complete grassing over will help to stimulate fruiting.

Pruning and After-care
A well-grown young tree will have three or four main branches so that 1-year-old wood – that is, the newer growth – should be cut back half-way, to an outward-facing bud. Strong shoots may be cut less hard, i.e. less far back, and the weaker branches rather harder, i.e. further back. The following autumn or winter the new growth is treated in the same way.

Keep the best two or three shoots that come from the original branches – that is the leaders – and cut out any shoots that cross the centre of the tree. The aim is to encourage a cup-shaped framework of branches.

In the following years treat the main shoots in the same way. Meanwhile, the main branches will have grown side shoots – laterals – and those that grow outwards from the tree can be left their full length. But those growing inwards will need to be cut back each winter to two buds from the base.

To keep a healthy atmosphere around the base of the tree plant chives and other herbs. Add a 2 gallon (9 l) mulch of compost each year. Young apple trees will need regular watering during a very dry period.

Pollination
Pollination requires consideration when it comes to choosing the varieties of apple for the garden. Varieties may be diploids or triploids. With diploids the pollen germinates readily; but with triploids the germination is very poor. Being poor pollinators, triploids should not be grown to cross-pollinate other varieties. If a triploid is grown, it is necessary to grow two other varieties so that one can pollinate the triploid and they can pollinate each other. It is fortunate that triploids are few in number. The majority of varieties are diploids. Some are self-fertile too. When choosing two varieties it is essential that they flower at the same time so that cross-pollination is assured. There are some varieties which set most fruits with their pollen but will benefit when cross-pollinated and give better and more regular crops. It is therefore advisable to interplant all varieties of apples. Another useful tip is to plant a variety of crab apple such as John Downie or Golden Hornet, for pollination of apples flowering in mid-season.

Selection of Dessert Apples
George Cave. A good-quality early and well-flavoured dessert apple. Bright yellow, flushed and striped red. A tree of moderate growth; regular and heavy cropper. When pruning, the laterals should be cut back to 5 or 6 buds in the winter. Pollinators are Worcester Pearmain, Egremont Russet, Laxtons Fortune and James Grieve. July–August ripening. This variety would make a change from the usual commercial varieties.

Laxton's Fortune. Makes a small compact tree suitable for the small garden. Fruit pale yellow with long red stripes and flushed red. Firm, crisp, sweet with a rich flavour. Pollinators are: George Cave, Arthur Turner, Egremont Russet, James Grieve and Lord Lambourne. Crops heavily when cross-pollinated. Mid-season flowering. September–October ripening.

Egremont Russet. An upright, compact and well-spurred tree, and considered one of the best dessert apples. Popular for small gardens and very suitable for northern areas. Excellent flavour. Pollinators Laxton's Fortune, James Grieve and Arthur Turner. Early flowering. October–November ripening.

Lord Lambourne. Regarded as one of the best of garden apples, being reliable and disease-resistant with the hardiness of its parent, James Grieve. It is a regular cropper, and a variety recommended for flavour and quality. Does well under conditions of high rainfall and humidity. Medium-sized fruit with greenish-yellow skin with crimson flush. Flesh is sweet and juicy. Early flowering. October–November ripening. An excellent pollinator for all early-flowering apples.

Sunset. A Cox type apple, now widely planted in less favourable areas. Crops well in a heavy type soil. Fruit has an orange russeted skin. Flesh very firm. Excellent flavour and keeps well. Mid-season flowering. Season: October–December.

Other dessert apples suitable for a small garden include Ellison's Orange, Golden Delicious, Granny Smith, James Grieve and Cox's Orange Pippin.

Selection of Cooking Apples

Lane's Prince Albert. Makes a small weeping tree, suitable for a small garden. Because of its drooping habit, laterals need to be pruned back to an upward-pointing bud and, as the fruit is borne on spurs of medium length, pruned to five or six buds during the winter. Useful in gardens subject to late frosts. Mid-season flowering. Crops well with large green fruit striped red. Best used December to March. Pollinators include Worcester Pearmain, Ellison's Orange, Cox's Orange Pippin, Laxton's Superb and Newton Wonder. It is partly self-compatible and remains in flower over a long period.

Newton Wonder. Very late cooking apple, ripening November and keeping in natural storage into March. Large fruit of high quality, yellow-fleshed crimson skin and firm flesh. A very vigorous tree and a heavy cropper when cross-pollinated. Pollinators include Worcester Pearmain, Ellison's Orange, Cox's Orange Pippin and Laxton's Superb. Has fruit borne on spurs of medium length, so laterals need to be pruned back to five or six buds in the winter.

Bramley's Seedling. The favourite cooker for baking and stewing. Large to very large flat fruit, green with red flush. A strong grower and comes into bearing early on dwarfing stock Malling 9. A triploid, so two pollinators are required. Worcester Pearmain, Arthur Turner, Ellison's Orange, Lane's Prince Albert, Laxton's Superb, Cox's Orange Pippin and Newton Wonder are suitable. It is a tip bearer so in the first years laterals should not be shortened too much. Pruning should consist of thinning out overcrowding and crossing laterals. If picked in October it will keep in natural storage until April.

Grenadier. Makes a compact tree useful for small gardens and comes quickly into bearing. It crops well in a wet clay soil and is resistant to scab. It is a good cropper with medium- to large-sized fruit, which are conical in shape, green, with a slight red flush. It is best to begin using the fruit before they are fully ripe, as they do not keep well after falling. Pollinators include Early Victoria, Lane's Prince Albert, and James Grieve. Season: August–September.

The above is a limited list selected for the home garden. If you need to store apples it is best to pick them on a dry day and then only those which are unblemished. Apples need a cool airy place. It is best to keep each fruit in special oiled paper in a single layer in a tray. Apples which have fallen from the tree and become bruised can go on the compost heap.

Pears

The pear is noted for its juicy consistency and fine flavour. It is virtually trouble-free and always well worth growing. Though the best pears are produced on loams, they are fairly tolerant of most soils, and because they dislike drought, watering during a dry summer is important.

Being somewhat early flowering means pears are also vulnerable to frost damage, something to be borne in mind when choosing a site.

A few pears, but none of the ones listed here, are triploids and some others are incompatible in specific combinations, so take care when selecting varieties.

If the soil is heavy clay it is advisable to prepare it well in advance of planting time, applying a mulch of compost and sharp gritty sand to the proposed area.

The form and variety of tree to be grown depends on space available and whether the garden receives plenty of sun. Trees smaller than half-standards are grown grafted on quince stock, usually Malling A. This is perhaps too vigorous for some varieties, namely Beurré Hardy and Doyenné du Comice, and these are better grown on Malling C, a less vigorous stock. A bush type would be suitable for a small garden being less demanding, so far as pruning is concerned, than cordons, dwarf pyramids and espaliers. Most garden centres supply all these, normally sold in containers at 2 or 3 years old. Certain varieties are a bit more expensive because they are incompatible with quince stock, so a short stem from a compatible variety is grafted in to act as an 'intermediate' between them. Cordons require posts and wires, but in a

garden of limited space a few could be planted by a south- or west-facing close board fence or wall.

Pears that are to be grown in grass need to be half-standards or larger if they are to give any headroom under them. These are best grafted on to seedling pear stock.

Soil Preparation and Planting

It is better to prepare the soil for planting well in advance even on a good loam. The soil must be bare of all growth for at least as far as the branches extend. In grass, pears need more space than apples, so follow the same directions as for planting apples, remembering to plant level with the soil mark on the stem, and to see that the union between the scion and rootstock is about 3 inches (75 cm) above soil level. Keep the soil area surrounding the tree well watered, especially during a dry summer.

Feeding

Pears will need to be fed each year, preferably in early February, by applying 2 bucketsful of veganic compost around the base within a circle 2 to 3 feet (60 cm to 90 cm) across in the first year. In the second and subsequent years spread three bucketsful of compost over an area equivalent to that covered by the tree's branches. Supplement this annually with 8 oz (225 g) of bonfire ashes.

Pruning

The pruning of pears in the early stages follows a similar pattern to that of apples. Pears will in the main stand harder pruning than apples.

Encourage a bush tree to form a sturdy framework of branches by only moderately pruning during the early years. Three or four branches can then be pruned to produce between 6 and 8 branches from two well-positioned buds; this method can then be repeated for the following year.

A basic framework having been established, pruning should be lighter until the tree begins to bear fruit. Pears tend to spur up more easily than apples, and it will only be necessary to thin out the spur system once the tree has started to crop, and this will encourage new wood growth.

Varieties

Williams Bon Chrétien (dessert). A well-known pear of high quality. A very good choice for gardens and is suitable for cold areas. Ready for picking during early September and ripening indoors. The long fruits are yellow with faint red stripes when ripe. A heavy and reliable cropper. Pollinators include Beurré Hardy, Conference and Doyenne du Comice. Needs to be double-worked onto rootstock.

Conference (dessert). Will succeed almost anywhere. It is a tree of only moderate vigour, and if on quince, the rootstock will be highly productive. It is self-fertile but it is always a good idea to have another variety such as Williams Bon Chrétien or Beurré Hardy as this will ensure the fullest possible germination. Conference is a mid-season flowering pear. The flavour is very good and the pulp is sweet and juicy, making a first-class fruit. Normally picked during the second half of September and ready for use during the second half of October and through November.

Doyenne du Comice (dessert). Introduced into England from France in 1858, this must be one of the best-flavoured dessert pears. Provided it is planted in a warm, favoured position and given suitable pollination, cropping will be regular and satisfactory. Fruit is sweet, juicy, melting and delicious. Picking is from the first week in October and at intervals into November. Good pollinators are Williams Bon Chrétien, Conference and Glou Morceau (Beurré de Hardenpont). Keeps well in natural storage until end of December.

Dr Jules Guyot (dessert). A good variety of pear for less-favoured gardens as it flowers late and normally produces a heavy crop. It must be picked at the right time and it may even be necessary to pick over the tree more than once, otherwise the fruit will be of poor quality. It is an excellent pollinator for other varieties. Good pollinators are Beurré Hardy, Conference, Doyenne du Comice and Glou Morceau. Needs to be double-worked onto rootstock.

Beurré Hardy (dessert). Makes a fairly large tree so space is needed where it can be allowed to grow as it is rather spreading. Flowers late in season; fruits best picked before they part readily from the tree. Large russeted fruit ripens with a red flush. Excellent flavour. Season: October.

Hessle (dessert). A very old variety said to grow almost anywhere, although its vigorous growth may make it unsuitable for a small garden or any but the poorest soil. A regular and heavy cropper with small, greenish, partly russeted, sweet and juicy fruit. Late flowering and partly self-fertile. Pick in the last week of September and use in October.

CHAPTER 12

GROWING UNDER GLASS

Growing certain crops under glass has many advantages. With such aids as cold frames, cloches or greenhouses, the season can extend for lettuce and other salad crops, including in particular tomatoes and cucumbers. Melons can be grown and most if not all hardy or semi-hardy garden vegetables given useful protection from the harsher features of the British climate, particularly in their younger stages. Yields are earlier and larger and hence better use is made of time and space. It is important to assess the best place in the garden for a cold frame and/or small greenhouse to sit, as ample sun and light are important for growing under glass; if possible the site should be within an area already down to vegetables and soft fruit.

Also to be considered are whether the site is protected with an adequate fence and gates, how much water is available, how close the place is to your home, and whether time is available as needed during the season for ventilating, watering and feeding the crops. All these factors need to be carefully thought about before embarking on growing under glass, particularly on an allotment, while arrangements need to be made when holidays come around because of the watering and ventilating involved, especially with tomatoes and cucumbers.

The watering of crops under cloches, cold frames, and in the greenhouse is important as soils can so easily dry out under glass, particularly during the summer period. All in all, a home garden is more likely to be a better place for a greenhouse and/or cold frame than is an allotment, on the basis that the single most important factor is the all-round health and well-being of the crops. There are on the market a vast range of cloches, cold frames and greenhouses available in varying sizes to suit most requirements and pockets. Let us look at the respective merits of each type of glass protection for crops.

Cloches

Cloches are designed to help protect germinating seeds and plants from the effects of cold winds, heavy rains and to some extent from frost. For many years, 'continuous cloches' as they were named were very popular, and to a certain degree they are still used. Today the types of protection offered by the more static garden frame and cold (unheated) greenhouse are proving more popular, but even so a few cloches can be extremely useful, particularly in conjunction with a few Dutch lights on a frame bed unit.

Continuous cloches consist of two types – the tent (consisting of two panes of glass) and the barn (four panes of glass). The cloches are placed end to end touching one another in rows so as to form a continuous range. The end of the ranges may be closed by a sheet of glass held in position by a stake. There is always ventilaton because of the small spaces between the sheets of glass. Such cloches are simply constructed, portable, and can be fairly easily dismantled and packed away in a small space such as at the end of a garden bed when not in use. Their chief value is probably that seedlings and plants are protected against excessive rain and strong winds while still being able to receive maximum light, especially early in the season. However, like all man-made things, cloches possess not only advantages (already mentioned) but disadvantages, such as the panes of glass being easily breakable, the possibility of catching them when working among them, and the need to open each one to provide extra ventilation on a hot day and having to move them when weeding and watering.

A particular advantage of the veganic system to the cloche user is the very great convenience of the raised beds, 4 feet 6 inches (1.37 m) wide. Both the tent and barn types can be accommodated in two rows with a 2 inch (5 cm) gap down the centre of the bed and 2 inches (5 cm) soil space on each side of the outer glass of the cloches.

This is enough exposed soil to allow the penetration of rain into the side areas of each cloche, although in dry periods watering will need to be carried out in order to make sure the whole span of soil underneath each cloche is adequately moist apart from the narrow areas next to the glass edges. Also, with the raised beds and pathways any breakages from accidental kicking or trampling will be far less frequent than when the cloches are simply on the flat, where it is extremely easy to catch their edges and corners.

Cloches may be used to cover as many as four successive crops every season, although one needs to start the growing season early and end it late to do this. Usually each crop will be cloched for only the initial stages of growth, and will then mature in the open, the cloches being moved on to the next crop.

All salad crops can be grown under cloches: and outdoor tomatoes can be protected by standing two cloches on their end and surrounding each plant, until quite late in the season.

To assist the ripening of the fruits the plants may be laid down on clean dry straw or peat and re-covered with cloches from September onwards.

With outdoor ridge cucumbers the seed may be sown the first week in May, and germination is hastened if the proposed area is covered with a cloche or cloches a few weeks before sowing. These are just a few of the many ways in which cloches can be utilized.

The Cold Frame
All salad crops such as lettuce, radish, carrots and spring onions can be grown successfully in a cold frame, during the spring period. Then, from mid-May onwards, cucumbers and melons can occupy the frame until September, after which it can be prepared for autumn sowings of spring lettuce, carrots and onions, with radishes sown then and again in January. Young tomato plants will benefit from having protection for a short period under glass after which the frame cover is removed to give the plants the benefit of the summer weather.

Although there is a wide choice in cold frames, the Dutch light is probably the most useful type to acquire. The Dutch light is simple and efficient, easily handled and relatively cheap. It can be added to indefinitely as more space and/or funds become available. It is possible to have more supports than lights and so move the lights on from a maturing crop to an immature one, a very useful facility.

The names of suppliers are on page 139. You could, of course, make your own. The light itself (see picture 21) consists of a single sheet of horticultural glass 55½ by 28¾ inches (141 cm by 73.5 cm) which slides into grooves in a timber surround. The timber is red deal or western red cedar and is normally pressure-treated and unpainted. A single-span unit can consist of one or more lights. Please refer to pages 134–136 for list of materials and how to erect a Dutch frame bed unit to take four Dutch lights.

The Dutch light unit should stand on a level or slightly sloping site and, so that the plants receive ample sun and light, particularly in the early months of the year, should face south or as near south as possible. (Large, double-span units, with two banks of lights sharing a common central flat top rail on posts, such as are found mainly on commercial holdings, are sited with the ridge running north to south.)

Set the frame unit on a 5-foot-wide (1.5 m wide) bed with a 2-foot-wide (61 cm wide) path at the front, with a similar path, if there is space, at the back.

The soil is cleared and prepared in exactly the same way as for outdoor strip garden beds. First the back boards and the side triangles are put in position, then the 5 inch (130 mm) by 2 inch (50 mm) timber for the bottom front rail.

The actual Dutch lights will go on the frame unit once the soil has been prepared for seed-sowing or planting. Any work carried out is done from the pathways as for open beds, assuming there is a path at the rear of the frame unit as well. Otherwise, any work can be done from a piece of 9 inch by 1 inch (23 cm by 2.5 cm) board about 6 feet

Picture 21 Dutch lights in place on a cold frame unit. Props of different lengths can be used to facilitate ventilation, weeding, watering and so on.

(1.8 m) long placed on the back and bottom front rails (see plate 5). Once the Dutch lights are in position, the watering, weeding, etc., can be done with one light raised at a time using a prop (see plate 5a).

When needing to ventilate the Dutch lights on the frame unit, then use one wooden block for each light. Each block (see picture 21) is 8 inches by 4 inches by 2 inches (200 mm by 100 mm by 50 mm) and for easy reference the following terms are used:

High = 8 inches (200 mm)
Mid = 4 inches (100 mm)
Low = 2 inches (50 mm)

To ventilate, lift the lower end of a Dutch light with the left hand and place a block centrally on the bottom front rail.

Lettuce (Autumn Sowing)

Assuming a single-span unit has been set up by early October and the soil prepared by the same routine as for outdoor garden beds, then after a thorough watering, especially on a light or medium well-draining soil, veganic seed-sowing compost mixture is spread over the area required for lettuce ten days before seed sowing. After ten days (it will now be mid-October) scrap the soil and rake level, and make shallow indentations with the back of the rake or a marking cane, from the back rail to the front or if you prefer, across with 9 inches (23 cm) between them, approximately ¼ to ½ inch (6 mm to 12 mm) deep. Then drop three or four lettuce seed at 4½ inch (115 mm) stations along the rows, brush the soil to cover them with the back of the hand, and firm with the presser.

After a few days give the Dutch light unit some low ventilation using wooden blocks. When the lettuce has germinated, keep the frame ventilated during any warm spells to ensure sturdy seedlings. There will not be any significant growth during December or January. Test the soil under the Dutch lights and, if it is dry, give a little water between the rows of lettuce seedlings. Thin out the seedlings to one every 4½ inches (115 mm), once they have grown their first true leaves. One Dutch light will yield twenty-four lettuces at 9 by 9 inches (23 cm by 23 cm) spacing, which under normal conditions should mature at the end of March and during early April, depending on variety. When the leaves touch, remove every other lettuce – these will be about half-size – as saladings, leaving the remainder to grow on to maturity.

If the weather is open in January, early carrot seed may be sown between the rows of growing lettuce. In February, begin feeding with diluted seaweed solution at fourteen-day intervals, at the rate of ⅔ gallon (3 l) for every twenty-four lettuces. Remove any weeds which may have grown with the aid of the scrapper and draw the point of the tool about 1 inch (2.5 cm) deep between the rows of lettuce, unless carrots have been sown.

It is important that the soil under Dutch lights remains moist and not completely dry as lettuce need moisture to ensure rapid and even growth to mature well. On the other hand, try to avoid wetting lettuce leaves when watering.

Varieties for Growing Under Dutch Lights
The best lettuce for October sowing is the Dutch variety, Kloek, producing fine large heads by the end of March and early April. Another to be recommended is Kwiek, which can be sown in late August and could well be ready during late November or early December, depending on weather. If sown in mid-October, Kwiek will also mature the following March/April.

Radishes
A big advantage of some kind of cold frame is that an early sowing of radish can be carried out in late January and early February even when the weather is bad.

The soil is prepared just as for outdoor sowings, except that the veganic seed compost can be applied ten days before sowing instead of twelve to fourteen days. Make sure the soil is clear of weeds and is moist before applying the seed compost.

Rake the soil well after ten days and sow the radish seed very thinly, and if possible at ½ inch (12 mm) between seeds in rows 4 inches (10 cm) apart, either across the Dutch light area or from front to back. Cover the seed by brushing soil over the rows with the back of the hand and firm well with the presser.

Remove any weeds which may have grown due to the slightly warmer conditions under the Dutch light, and where necessary thin out the radishes to the half-inch spacing at the same time. Give at least one liquid feed of seaweed solution. A further sowing may be made within a week.

First sowings can be of the variety Scarlet Globe or Cherry Belle, followed by Sparkler and French Breakfast at seven-to-ten day intervals. It is a good idea to use half a Dutch light area for each sowing. Give a little ventilation for an hour or two during the middle of the day should the weather be fine and dry. Always keep the soil moist for radish growing.

Carrots

The growing of young carrots under cold frames or cloches can be very rewarding. There are two dates for sowing: early October for pulling in January/February, and early January for pulling in April/May.

For the October sowing the lights should be removed from the frame unit in mid-September in order to prepare the soil by the normal routine already described, making sure the soil is moist when applying a seed compost mixture. Replace the lights and then in early October either remove or raise and prop one in order to carry out the sowing. Rake the soil well and mark rows 5 inches (12.5 cm) apart using either the back of the rake or a marking cane to make slight indentations. The depressions need to be ½ inch to ¾ inch (12 mm to 20 mm) deep. Sow very thinly and then brush the soil over the seeds with the back of the hand or the back of the rake, and then firm the soil well with the presser board. (The routine is the same as for outdoor sowing of carrots.)

Keep the Dutch light frame unit closed for two or three days, then give a gentle mist-spray with water during the morning. Give a little ventilation for a few hours if the weather is open. Then follow the same routine as for outdoor carrots regarding thinning and weed-ing, bearing in mind that, being under glass, they will from time to time require to be ventilated.

After thinning – and it is best to do this on a dull day – give them a feed of liquid seaweed solution every fourteen days.

For the early January sowing the Dutch lights will need to be removed in mid-December to facilitate the work of clearing the soil, by scrapping in the usual manner and applying the seed-sowing compost mixture. Replace the lights after sowing.

Then again follow the routine as for outdoor carrots. With daylight hours increasing more markedly from February onwards, it is essential to keep the frame ventilated during spells of dry and fine weather. It is also important that the soil never dries out.

As already mentioned, lettuce can be intercropped with carrots under the same Dutch light or cold frame, and carrots can also be intercropped with radish.

Varieties

Suitable varieties for sowing in either early January or October under glass include the following:

Early Nantes. Excellent for successful sowings under Dutch lights and cloches.

Amsterdam Forcing. One of the best for early sowings under glass.

Cucumbers

Cucumbers grown under Dutch lights during the summer can be most success-ful as they can then have the space they need, their growth being quite exten-sive.

Soil Preparation and Planting

If there has been a crop of lettuce or radish growing under the Dutch lights over the winter period then, usually during late April, remove the lights and clean and prepare the soil in the usual way.

Be sure to remove, using the scrapper, all the stubs of lettuce and any weeds which may have grown during the final few days of the lettuce maturing. Water well the 'top' half of the area of soil of the frame unit (i.e. the back half), and apply a gallon (4.5 l) of veganic compost mixed with a generous handful of sharp gritty sand in a disc about 8 inches (20 cm) in diameter, with its centre just above half-way across the Dutch light soil area from the front.

Planting can be carried out from the middle of May to the end of the month. Purchase well-grown sturdy cucumber plants grown in pots by a reliable plant grower or garden centre.

With the planting knife make a hole big enough to accommodate the whole of the plant root and work into this hole some of the compost which has already been applied previously. After planting make a slight mound up to the plant stem, so that water will percolate rapidly into the soil surrounding the plant. As a precaution against burning by the sun after planting, place a sheet of newspaper over the plant to prevent scorching when the light or lights are replaced. Within a short time it will be necessary to apply whitewash or some other shading to the glass to prevent scorching the leaves.

Ventilation and Training the Plant
Keep the frame closed for two days after planting, then give a little ventilation from mid-day for a few hours, closing down the frame at between 3 and 4 p.m.

The cucumber needs a hot but humid atmosphere in order to flourish and produce a good crop, but a little ventilation is necessary to maintain a healthy plant during its growth, especially when the main laterals and sub-laterals are forming, as these soon cover the soil area under the Dutch lights.

When about five or six rough-edged cucumber leaves have formed then pinch out the main growing point of the plant; this encourages the growth of laterals, these are the main ones, but it is on the sub-laterals that fruit is allowed to form. Usually about four or five main laterals grow; when these are about 18 inches (45 cm) long, stop and pinch out the growing point of each. When two or three fruits have formed on each sub-lateral, pinch out the growing point of each of these. Always remove any small cucumber which has grown on the main stem or a main lateral, as failure to do this will result in a reduced crop. Also keep a sharp look out for male flowers and pinch all of them out from the plant as the cucumber must remain female to be sweet tasting, once pollinated, it will be decidedly bitter.

It will be necessary to protect each cucumber from soil damage by placing under it a small tile or piece of wood, approximately 9 inches by 4 inches (23 cm by 10 cm), to keep it dry and clean.

Watering and Feeding
Make sure the plants are liberally watered and give a mist spray with water before closing the frame down between 3 and 4 p.m. During the summer, give a liquid feed of seaweed solution every fourteen days at the rate of 1 gallon (2.2 l) to each plant and apply a further mulch of veganic compost around the centre of the plant every three or four weeks.

Because of the attention cucumbers, let alone melons, require, it can be readily appreciated why it is better to have a cold frame in the home garden rather than at the allotment.

Varieties

Telegraph Improved. Reliable cropper. Smooth fruits of good length.

Butcher's Disease Resisting. Produces a good crop, disease-resisting fruit, slightly ribbed, of medium size.

There are a number of varieties of cucumbers which are all-female, so saving work on having to remove the male flowers, but under certain conditions of stress, male flowers may nevertheless appear, and will have to be removed.

Melons

Another rewarding crop to grow in a cold frame is the melon, and it will pay to give this attractive and sweet-tasting fruit the extra attention it requires.

The soil preparation and planting is exactly the same as for cucumbers, and the time for planting under a cold frame, cloche or Dutch light is again between the middle of May and the end of the month.

Ventilation

Ventilation during the growth of the melon differs from the ventilation of the cucumber. After planting, cover each plant with a sheet of newspaper or some equivalent, to protect against the sun until it has become established and keep the frame closed for two or three days, unless the sun is very strong, when slight ventilation should be given, but close the frame down around 4 p.m.

During growth the ventilation will need to be increased from 'mid' to 'high' on most sunny days. The air under the frame should be drier than for cucumbers and more buoyant.

It is as well to apply a coat of whitewash or other suitable shading to the glass over the centre of the plant to prevent leaf scorch.

Training and Pollinating Melon Plants

When the main stem of the plant has formed shoots for three of four main laterals, cut out the growing point from the main stem. This will encourage both the main and the sub-laterals to grow more rapidly. Be sure to do any cutting of stems with a very sharp knife.

From the three or four main laterals there will grow sub-laterals and on these the fruits will form. Each melon plant produces two kinds of flowers, male and female. The female flowers can be distinguished by a small green swelling at the base of the flower below the petals. The male flowers are more in number and bear the pollen. For fertilizing, the pollen must be transferred from the male to the female flowers. This may be done by bees during the hot weather, when the bees will be out and the frames open, but otherwise you will have to pick a perfectly formed and even-petalled male flower, strip the petals from it and then gently rub its pollen onto the stigma of the open female flowers. As far as possible, all mature flowers on a plant should be pollinated on the same day.

In a few days, evidence of fertilization of some of the female flowers will be seen in the increase in size of the small green swellings behind the petals. When these are about the size of a walnut, the most evenly formed ones are selected and retained to produce the fruit.

The remainder are removed, including any on the main stem. Depending on the variety, it is usual to allow at least four melons per plant – more on the cantaloupe melon type. The main laterals will need to be stopped, the fruit-bearing sub-laterals shortened to two leaves above the fruit and other shoots thinned out periodically. Over-thinning should be avoided as there must be sufficient leaves retained to assist in fruit development. Excessive foliage tends to exhaust the plant.

Watering and feeding

Watering of melons is not so lavish as for cucumbers, but it must be done carefully as melons dislike too much water at any time. The plants are, if anything, kept on the dry side during the early growing period, and particularly on dull cold days, care being taken at all times to keep any water away from the actual main central stem. When the fruits are developing rapidly, a reasonable supply of water is given until the fruits ripen, when less water is given. After about the fourth week give a mulch of veganic compost (double handful) and at fourteen-day intervals give a liquid feed of seaweed solution at the rate of ½ gallon (2.2 l) per plant.

It is better to water in the early morning so there is no free moisture present when the temperature falls in the evening. In addition syringe the foliage frequently during favourable weather until the fruits begin to ripen or 'net'.

Keep the frame area weeded, but during the last two weeks of the melons ripening simply ignore any weed growth, except any tall weeds which may have been missed earlier.

Each fruit should be raised off the frame bed soil by means of a tile or small piece of wood 6 inches (15 cm) square to keep it dry and clean. Melons are ready for cutting when the actual stalk cap is coming away, making cracks around it.

Varieties of Ordinary Melon

Blenheim orange. Very succulent, orange flesh; medium size.

Hero of Lockinge. White-fleshed.

Varieties of Cantaloupe Melon

Sweetheart (F_1 hybrid). Medium-sized fruits, light orange flesh; one of the earliest to ripen.

Early Sweet (F_1 hybrid). Round fruits with a netted skin; deep salmon-pink flesh, sweet and well-flavoured.

Ogen. Small round fruits with a yellow-green flesh, very sweet and fine flavour.

The Unheated Greenhouse

Growing some early salad crops, also tomatoes, sweet peppers and melons in a cold greenhouse can be very rewarding, while the benefit also of being able to do a little gardening under cover, in the dry, when outside is anything but pleasant, must surely be an added bonus.

At the same time, following the veganic system will ensure that the texture and productiveness of the greenhouse soil are improved rapidly and with little effort. Furthermore, the whole atmosphere within the structure will be a clean and pleasant one in which to work.

For anyone contemplating the purchase of a small greenhouse the best possible place needs to be chosen in the garden, so that there is the maximum light for the growing plants, especially during the late winter and early spring period. This means choosing a site well away from overhanging trees and yet so positioned that the greenhouse can be an attractive feature which will blend in with the overall garden theme.

Here the type and size of structure needs to be carefully considered, as the appearance of a small greenhouse in a garden is an important element, particularly if it is in view from the house. A greenhouse constructed of wood has its attractions provided it is stained regularly. Many garden centres have a wide range of both timber and aluminium alloy ones on sale.

One type of timber house is the Dutch light greenhouse. This is made of a chosen number of wooden-framed single-pane lights which are bolted together with sides which slope outwards at the base, thus allowing the maximum amount of daylight to enter.

Several models are equipped with sliding doors. These greenhouses are very strong, being braced internally, although it is important that the bracing timbers should not impede plant growth or easy working.

Ventilation is another important aspect, just as with cold frames. With a Dutch light house ventilation in both roof and sides is normal. Another advantage of this type is that glazing is dry; the glass slides into grooves of the frames. This allows more air exchange within even when there is no other ventilation.

There must also be a source of water near the greenhouse site. Always remember that greenhouse crops get no normal rainfall, while the soil tends to dry out faster despite the lack of wind. Plants growing in a greenhouse must be watered regularly.

Forming raised soil beds inside the greenhouse

If there happen to be a fair quantity of weeds, either annual or deep-rooted, where the greenhouse is to be sited then these will need to be cleared by following the directions in Chapter 6.

The positioning of the greenhouse with its ridge running east to west takes full advantage of the available daylight during the winter months. With a Dutch light house with glass virtually down to the ground, the ridge can run north to south; this orientation would certainly help tomatoes or cucumbers or melons to receive a more even share of the sun during the summer months. The main thing is to avoid having the door facing into the prevailing wind. If the greenhouse roof ridge runs north to south, or nearly so, the raised soil beds should too. For a greenhouse with its ridge east–west, then the beds should be in the same direction. There may need to be certain adjustments made, as for instance in the actual width of the beds. For example, if the greenhouse is 8 feet (2.4 m) in length and 6 feet (1.8 m) in width, then have a pathway down the centre lengthwise – this can be 16 inches (41 cm) wide, and a bed each side approximately 2 feet 4 inches (71 cm) wide (see picture 22). The path may be strawed or made up of slabs.

Another example, and this applies particularly to a Dutch light greenhouse with a width of 11 feet (3.38 m), would mean a central bed 4 feet (1.2 m) wide, with a 15 inch (38 cm) wide pathway

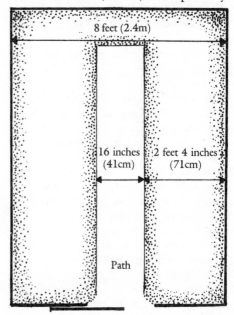

Picture 22 Example of layout of raised soil beds and path in a greenhouse 8 feet (2.4m) long.

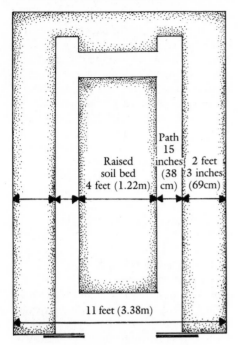

Path
15
inches
(38
cm)

2 feet
3 inches
(69cm)

Raised
soil bed
4 feet (1.22m)

11 feet (3.38m)

Picture 23 Example of how to set out raised soil beds and paths in a greenhouse 11 feet (3.38m) wide.

each side, leaving two narrow side beds 2 feet 3 inches (75 cm) wide (see picture 23).

A general rule to adopt for a layout inside a greenhouse is for a minimum width of path to be 12 inches (30 cm) and a maximum and minimum bed width of 4 feet 6 inches and 2 feet 4 inches (1.37 m and 71 cm respectively). The maximum width of a side bed should be 2 feet 4 inches (71 cm).

Be sure to plan the layout in such a way as to enable an easy comfortable reach across a soil bed from a path without treading on the cropping soil.

When forming the beds, follow the directions given in Chapter 4, simply making any necessary adjustments as to width and soil depth according to soil type, and there is also the need to decide on the kind of material to cover the paths.

With the application of clean veganic compost each season there is no need to annually remove soil from the greenhouse or to sterilize or fumigate it.

Weeding
It is best to hand pull any weeds among tomatoes, cucumbers, melons, sweet peppers and aubergine to prevent damage to the fine root hairs of each plant. To aid weed removal among lettuce, radish and carrots, the scrapper can be used.

Lettuce (Spring and Winter)
It is sound sense to make the fullest use of a cold greenhouse after the summer crops have finished, instead of leaving it empty during the winter. Lettuce is probably the most useful crop to grow, but some early carrots and radish can also be grown, thus providing a 'salad' as it were.

Lettuce need as much light as possible and one can appreciate the value of a glass-to-ground type greenhouse, particularly during the shorter and darker days of winter. It is important to remove and cut up all haulms of any previous summer crop, and put them on the compost heap. (The actual hard roots should go in a 'rough' heap or be burnt.) Tomatoes may well occupy a greenhouse well into October, but possibly there will be a small area free of any crop, which can be prepared for the earliest sowings of lettuce.

Scrap-weed the proposed area, water it well and leave overnight. If the area has been composted for any previous crop then seed can be sown immediately, otherwise spread the seed compost mixture on the area and leave for ten days. Then rake it well before sowing.

Use a marking cane or the back of a rake to make shallow indentations ½ inch (13 mm) deep and sow Kwiek seed thinly in three rows, 9 inches (23 cm) between the rows, and cover with soil by drawing it over the seed with back of hand or rake. Firm the soil with the presser board.

Thin out the seedlings to 4½ inches (12 cm) apart in the row when they have two true leaves, and begin feeding with seaweed solution repeating every fourteen days at the same rate as for outdoor lettuce.

Kwiek is an excellent large-headed variety. Sown in August, it should mature in November–December. A further sowing of Kwiek can be made in September or early October, which should mature sometime in March or early April.

The variety Kloek which produces fine large solid heads, could also be sown in mid-October and, given a reasonable winter, mature in late March or early April. Early carrots can be sown in October for pulling in January and February. Carrots sown in January can be ready for pulling in April–May. Follow the same routine as for cold-frame cropping as described earlier in the chapter, and do the same for radish, making sowings in autumn and January/February.

It is possible that lettuce will not quite achieve a full solid heart, and only produce a more loose type of head. Much depends on the daylight hours and outside weather conditions.

Tomatoes
The tomato is probably the most popular of the greenhouse salad crops to grow. A reasonably good crop can be obtained by growing the plants in a large container, but the most productive results are achieved by planting direct into the soil beds which allows for a freer root run.

Soil Preparation and Planting
Preparation of the soil is exactly the same as for all crops in the veganic system, and it is advisable to make sure of having sufficient compost available at planting time. For cold greenhouse cropping the month of May is ideal, mid-May being perhaps the safest and most suitable time.

If you are unable to raise tomato plants then purchase well-grown, sturdy and non-discoloured plants from the garden centre or local nurseryman.

Space them at 16 inches (41 cm) in the row and use a good double handful of compost in the hole with each. After planting, each plant will need to be supported and a bamboo cane 8 feet (2.4 m) in length can be pushed 1 or 1½ feet (30 to 45 cm) into the soil some 2 inches (5 cm) away from the plant, so as not to damage the roots. Use raffia for tying. Alternatively, soft fillis can be used instead of a cane by tying it firmly but not tightly to each stem base just below the first true leaf and fastening it to a wire stretched end to end overhead. Allow for the fillis to be twisted round the stem as the plant grows.

In the first year that tomatoes are grown in a cold greenhouse it is advisable to limit the trusses to six, but as the soil improves the number can be increased to seven or eight. On sunny days give some ventilation by opening the roof vent, and give a little side ventilation as well. Tomatoes require plenty of light and air in hot weather. To get a good set of tomatoes it is advisable to tap the flower clusters during a sunny morning or give a fine mist-spray of water at high pressure onto the plants between 10.30 and 11.30 a.m.

Take off ('pinch out') the side shoots (axils) when they are about an inch (2.5 cm) long, into the weed box, and if during growth any lower leaves turn yellow, remove these too. Remove any weed growth by hand.

Watering and Feeding
When the first truss is well formed it is time to apply a mulch of veganic compost to a moist soil, the amount being the same as for outdoor plants, namely a 2 gallon (9 l) bucketful for six plants.

At the same time, liquid feed with compost water or seaweed solution every ten days at the rate of 6 l to every six plants. Tomatoes respond well to liquid feeds. Keep up regular watering and feeding throughout the plant's growth.

Varieties
Moneymaker. Very reliable. Roundish fruits of medium size.

Alicante. Moneymaker type, excellent for cold greenhouses. Extremely reliable since it is remarkably resistant to lower temperatures. Medium fruits of fine flavour.

Ailsa Craig. Another reliable cropper, medium-sized fruits of good flavour.

There are a number of F_1 hybrid varieties which include Eurocross and Red Ensign; they grow vigorously with large, good quality, finely flavoured fruits. Seeds from F_1 hybrid should never be saved as their characteristics will vary from their parents.

Cucumbers
Cucumbers revel in hot and humid conditions. They need a rich soil which is well drained and ample water with liquid feeds. Generally, cucumbers need to be grown separately from tomatoes, which need a more buoyant atmosphere, but anyone especially keen to have both in the same greenhouse can achieve this by planting the cucumbers at the end of the greenhouse with a clear polythene sheet fixed in front of the plants so as to create a humid atmosphere round them. The polythene must be arranged so as to allow training and watering, etc., to be carried out. This situation is also helped with the newer varieties available today which are 'all-female' F_1 hybrid types. Cucumbers must remain female, otherwise when pollinated and grown on they will be very bitter to taste. All-female plants have no male flowers to be removed and hence need less access than those which do.

Soil Preparation and Planting
The soil for cucumbers is cleared in the usual manner described in Chapter 3. Where each plant is to be sited make up a mound with a mixture of 1 gallon (4.5 l) of soil to 2 gallons (9 l) of veganic compost at least three or four days beforehand. If more than one cucumber is grown then another soil/compost mound will need to be formed at least 4 feet (1.2 m) away. Two plants should be adequate for the average family.

Obtain sturdy well-grown plants from the garden centre and plant out from mid-May to the end of the month.

It is essential to provide a good support system by using a strong 4 foot (1.2 m) bamboo cane pushed well into the soil to tie the growing plant stem to in the initial stages and to have a number of parallel galvanized wires 9 inches (23 cm) apart stretched across the width of the greenhouse, the first one about 3 feet (90 cm) from the ground. The top of the cane is fastened to this.

Training the Plant During Growth
Use raffia to tie the main stem to the cane, in the same manner as described for outdoor tomatoes (Chapter 8) and continue to do this as the stem grows. Remove all side shoots which develop

in the leaf axils up to the first horizontal wire, to give a clear stem with leaves but no side shoots up to about 3 feet (90 cm). Above this, train the side shoots (laterals) horizontally, alternately left and right, as they become long enough. When each lateral produces a female flower, pinch out its tip after two leaves, then when the shoots from the axils of these leaves in turn produce more female flowers these must be pinched out one leaf beyond and so on. When the main leading stem reaches a height of about 5 feet (1.5 m) then remove its growing tip. Remove any male flowers immediately they appear.

Watering and Feeding
It is important not to over-water, but a moist soil-and-compost mound needs to be maintained, and additional compost mulch applied when tiny white surface roots show through. Apply 1 gallon (4.5 l) of compost as a mulch and continue to give liquid feeds of either compost water or seaweed solution every fourteen days at the rate of 2 pints (1.2 l) per plant. It is wise to apply a coat of whitewash, flour and water, or a proprietary shading to protect the leaves from scorching by the sun and to ventilate when the temperature exceeds 80° F (26° C).

Damping down should be carried out each day, that is wetting the glass and the path adjacent to the cucumber plants; about ½ gallon (2.2 l) per plant should be sprinkled on the adjacent path from a watering can, fitted with a rose.

Varieties
All-female F₁ hybrids: Femina, Femspot.

Traditional varieties include:

Telegraph Improved. This has smooth fruits of good length and is a reliable cropper.

Butcher's Disease Resisting. This produces medium-sized slightly ribbed fruits.

Melons
Melons, like cucumbers, crop well in a cold greenhouse, and the growing and training is similar as well. Although seeds can be sown in 3 inch (75 cm) pots in early to mid-May in the greenhouse, which should enable the plants to be ready for planting out at the end of May, it is probably better to obtain well-grown melon plants from a garden centre.

The soil preparation forming the soil and compost mixture for planting in is the same as described earlier in this chapter (see page 000).

Plant each melon plant in the centre of the soil/compost mound, and when watering them in make sure to avoid wetting the base of the stem next to the soil to avoid stem rot.

If planting more than one plant set them at least 4 feet (1.2 m) apart.

Training and Ventilating
It is essential to have fixed in advance three or four horizontal galvanized wires 9 inches (23 cm) apart for training the plant on to. For upright support push a 4 foot (1.2 m) bamboo cane well into the ground within 2 or 3 inches (5 cm to 75 cm) of the main stem of the plant, and fasten this cane to the first wire which ought to be about 3 feet (90 cm) from the ground.

When the main central stem has grown to 5 feet (1.5 m) pinch out the growing point, and tie the side shoots (laterals) to the wires. When these have grown to 18 to 20 inches (45 cm to 50 cm) in length, pinch out the growing tips. Sub-laterals which grow from the laterals will produce most of the fruit, and these will need to be stopped three leaves beyond the fruit, the other shoots being removed as necessary.

Pollination must be carried out on a sunny day as described in the section dealing with melons under cold'frames. To obtain an even pollination of fruit it is best to pollinate at least six well-placed female flowers on the same day or the next day.

Maintain a reasonable temperature somewhere between 60 and 72° F (15 and 22° C) and ventilate on very hot days, damping the path down as well, as described for cucumbers. Also, shade the glass on the outside with whitewash or other suitable shade material to prevent leaf scorch.

Each plant can produce up to four good-sized fruits or six smaller ones.

Watering and Feeding
Apply 1 gallon (4.5 l) of veganic compost after four weeks and give liquid feeds of either compost water or seaweed solution every fourteen days at the rate of 2 pints (1.2 l) per plant. Always have the soil moist before applying either compost or the liquid feeds, and endeavour to keep the main stem near the soil dry to prevent stem rot. When the fruits are the size of small oranges, support each melon in a hammock of netting, which needs to be firmly attached to the supporting wires. As the fruits start to ripen, gradually reduce watering, and keep the ventilation open during the daytime. Pick the fruits when they are coloured and the characteristic ripe aroma is apparent.

Varieties
Much the same as for cold-frame growing. The variety Blenheim Orange Superlativa is an excellent one for a cold greenhouse, medium-sized with scarlet flesh and a 'netted' skin.

Finally when all the fruit has been picked remove all the stems and leaves of the melon plant to the compost straight away. This goes for all plant remains when each crop finishes in either the cold frame or greenhouse.

Capsicum (Sweet Pepper)
There are two groups of peppers, the sweet and the hot. The former is *Capsicum annuum* and the latter is *Capsicum haccatum,* known to most cooks as chilli. The hot type should not be grown in the same greenhouse as the sweet one and its culture is not discussed in this book as it is generally regarded as an exotic, not to mention being an acquired taste!

Sweet peppers are cylindrical in shape or rather rounded, and can be sliced for use in salads. Like the tomato, they are green and then undergo a change in colour to red when fully ripe, though there is one variety, Oshkosh, which is yellow. They are fairly easy to grow in an unheated greenhouse, or cold frame.

Sow seeds in small pots or a seed tray in March in a heated greenhouse or propagator in a temperature of 60° F to 65° F (16 to 18° C). Transplant them into larger pots when large enough to handle. Alternatively, purchase sturdy well-grown plants from a garden centre. In any case always syringe plants frequently with water, using the 'fine' rose on watering cane. Plant in May, about 2 feet (60 cm) apart in a row down one side of the greenhouse. Make a hole big enough to take the root and a generous handful of compost. Firm the soil well after planting. It is advisable to support each plant with a strong bamboo cane or stake 3 feet (90 cm) long pushed 12 inches (30 cm) into the soil as the swelling fruits can make for top heaviness. Use raffia to tie to the cane. For an average family, three or four plants are a good number to grow, bearing in mind that a well-grown plant will yield at least twenty fruits. To assist the fruits to set, syringe the flowers daily with water on a sunny day. Fertilization may not be very good during dull and cool weather. Capsicums appreciate warm moist conditions and, like tomatoes, need to be well watered regularly.

Apply 1 gallon (4.5 l) of veganic compost when the first fruits have set. Thereafter, apply a liquid feed of compost water or diluted seaweed solution every fourteen days, at the rate of 2 pints (1.1 l) per plant.

If the greenhouse is a very small one and will only take a few tomato plants, then a sweet pepper plant can be planted in a 9 inch (23 cm) diameter pot, containing 50 per cent ordinary garden soil and 50 per cent compost with a little sharp sand. Stand the pot just inside the greenhouse until early June, then later outside in a sheltered sunny position. Alternatively, the pot can be sunk into the ground outside and protected with two barn cloches stood on their ends. Support the cloches by pushing bamboo canes into the ground. Give liquid feeds as for inside growing.

Varieties
Early Prolific (F₁ hybrid). An excellent one for earliness and yield. Produces fruit of excellent quality, size and texture.

New Ace (F₁ hybrid). Another early and high yielding one.

Canape. A popular variety.

Worldbeater. This produces fruit in abundance. Best grown in a greenhouse or frame, but will also do well in a large pot outdoors and protected by cloches.

Aubergine (Eggplant)
These sun-loving vegetables are, like sweet peppers, becoming more popular.

The aubergine plant is somewhat tender, but with the newer types of hybrids are much easier to grow. Again like the capsicum they can be sown in March and the temperature needs to be around 65° F (18° C) for germination. It is probably better to buy plants from a garden centre, and plant them in a greenhouse towards the end of May. Set the plants out about 2 feet 6 inches (76 cm) apart in the row with a handful of compost to each plant. Gentle syringing using the 'fine' rose on the watering can will help the fruit to set, and it is best to do this on a sunny morning between 10.30 and 11.30, avoiding too high a temperature. Keep syringing the plants on warm sunny days. When the plants are 9 inches (23 cm,) high, pinch out the growing point to encourage branching. Later pinch out sideshoots at two leaves beyond the fruit. Support each plant with a 5 foot (1.5 m) stake pushed 12 inches (30 cm) into the ground and tie each plant with raffia. The plants will eventually reach a height of 3 feet (90 cm).

Apply 1 gallon (4.5 l) of veganic compost as a mulch to each plant once the fruits are beginning to form. Keep the plants well watered throughout the summer period and give liquid feeds of compost water or diluted seaweed solution every fourteen to twenty-one days at the rate of 2 pints (1.1 l) per plant. During dry weather the plants must not be allowed to lack moisture or the skins could split. Cut the fruits when they have a uniform, well-coloured and polished appearance.

Varieties
Dusky (F₁ hybrid). A very early variety with large oval glossy black fruits. Ideal for growing in a cold or slightly heated greenhouse.

Moneymaker (F₁ hybrid). Probably one of the best to grow in a cold greenhouse. Very early.

Long Purple. An excellent maincrop aubergine.

CHAPTER 13

GARDEN DESIGN

The aim of this chapter is to suggest ideas – with a little help from a few plans (see pictures 24, 25 and 26) – to create a pleasant and yet functional garden when starting a new plot or to improve an established garden.

Thus the descriptive list of trees, shrubs, ground cover and climbing plants is simply intended to assist in forming a basic planting framework within which the reader can add herbaceous perennials, roses, bulbs and bedding plants according to taste.

The following are basic guidelines to be borne in mind when contemplating the planning and creation of a veganic garden, combining ornamental, leisure and productive purposes.

1. Veganic techniques should be applied throughout the garden appropriate to both ornamental and productive plants. This means:
   – adding vegetable humus to the soil's surface;
   – surface cultivation (no digging);
   – 'stepping stones' in borders to avoid soil compaction;
   – natural control of weeds and their use.

2. The leisure and productive areas of the garden can be combined more readily under the veganic system, because of the more aesthetic qualities of the productive part of the veganic garden.
   – Fruits, herbs, nuts and certain vegetables can form an integral part of the ornamental section, e.g. mints, apple, hazel, sweet corn, etc.;
   – a pleasant and healthy atmosphere can be created within the whole garden.

3. In the planning of the basic garden framework the following points should be considered:
   – sunny and shade areas;
   – 'outdoor room' or 'rooms' – place to relax;
   – play areas;
   – formal or informal approach (this is a personal preference which affects the quality of the place);
   – 'wild' areas;
   – the main structure, i.e. hedges, spaces, trees, shrubs, etc.;
   – shelter for plants and people.

4. The lawn – do you need one? Alternatives.
   – size and function;
   – character: what kind of lawn? Long grass, meadow with flowers, fine lawn, hardwearing lawn;
   – clearing the area for a lawn;
   – a new lawn from turf;
   – a new lawn from seed.

5. Selection of plant material:
   – trees: ornamental, evergreen or deciduous; foliage; specimen; fruit.
   – hedging: evergreen or deciduous, foliage, flowering; berrying.
   – shrubs: evergreen or deciduous; hardy; perennials; roses; ground

cover; climbing plants; heathers; bulbs.
6. Hard elements – patio, terrace, paths:
   – materials: stone, brick paviors, granite sets, cobbles, concrete slabs, pea gravel.
7. Garden features:
   – pergola, seats, containers.

Veganic techniques

The surface cultivation techniques of the veganic system are used throughout the garden whether for clearing ground, cultivating the soil, growing vegetables, soft fruit or shrubs, or for tending ornamental areas. The no-digging method of cultivating the soil is of immense benefit, not only in terms of soil improvement but in the better control of weeds among plants. It goes without saying that less energy is required in maintaining any planted areas, especially after the first year.

Where any shrub and flower border is wider than 3 feet (90 cm) flattish stones or bricks (a few placed side by side) are inserted into the ground to stand on for cultivating or weeding, etc., or applying compost or liquid feed.

Vegetable compost is used for vegetable crops, while in the main for shrubs, ground-cover, etc., tree-leaf compost or leaf mould is used, although any surplus vegetable compost – even semi-mature – can also be used for shrubs, etc.

The method of making tree-leaf compost is described in Chapter 5. Note that any surplus grass mowings – and these will be plentifully available if there is a large expanse of lawn – form a most useful ingredient in tree-leaf compost making.

Combining Leisure and Productive Areas

The neat beds of healthy vegetables and strawed paths are appealing in them-selves, but particularly in a very small garden it may be desirable to emphasize the amenity part of the garden.

This need not mean the sacrifice of crop production, since many productive plants have sculptural or decorative qualities in addition to their food value. If these plants are incorporated into the amenity section of the garden it is possible to achieve the best of both worlds and have a garden which is apparently designed for visual attraction but also provides a range of fruit, nuts and vegetables for human consumption.

Apples, pears and cherries can all be attractive decorative trees. Hazel (cob-nuts and filberts) is a most attractive small tree or shrub which can form an excellent background screen plant in mass. When more mature it forms a specimen tree of rather 'Japanese' habit.

Peaches and nectarines are lovely wall shrubs and can be trained into fan shapes. There are many varieties of grape vines which are hardy in Britain and will clothe a wall or pergola. Blackberries, notably the thornless cut-leaved type, carry large fruit and make vigorous reliable climbers.

For quick effect, the red-flowered runner bean is a delightful plant for pergolas, fences and porches. Her-baceous plants can also be effective dual-purpose plants, and sweet corn can make a striking contribution; the globe artichoke opens out into a most attrac-tive flower and even the vegetables like broccoli and curly kale can be effective in conjunction with ornamentals.

The Basic Framework

In planning *any* garden it is essential to determine its orientation and that of the house.

Deep shadows at certain times of the year can look very attractive in the ornamental part of the garden, but will not necessarily suit fruits and veg-

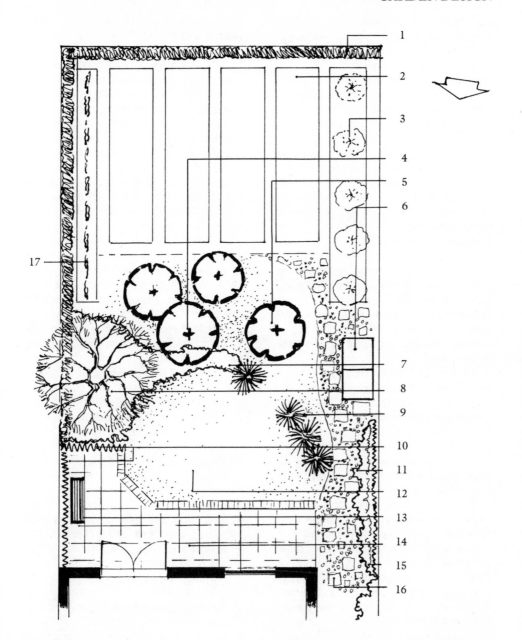

Picture 24 **Garden plan**
Key: 1 evergreen hedge; 2 no digging beds for salads and vegetables; 3 bush fruits; 4 three apples on dwarfing stock; 5 pear tree; 6 twin compost bin; 7 low ground cover plants; 8 deciduous ornamental tree; 9 conifer trees; 10 climbing plants; 11 herbs and climbing plants; 12 lawn; 13 seat; 14 paved patio with brick edging; 15 climbing plants; 16 paving in gravel; 17 cane and/or espalier fruit.

etables. So it pays to take note of where the sun will be during winter periods as well as in summertime. Also, remember that wind makes the garden uncomfortable for much of the year in some locations, and inhibits the growth of crops, so plan to make the best use of shelter areas or provide new shelter devices.

Many families enjoy sitting outdoors when the weather is fine, and this is where a paved area is most useful – in other words an extension of the house – an 'outdoor room' with possibly a pergola to train climbers on, can be practical and decorative.

A combination of your own taste and the site will determine whether the garden as a whole should be formal – that is, with flower and shrub borders surrounding a rectangular or square lawn, or informal with curved lawns and borders, and perhaps a small area to be left 'wild'.

All these matters will need to be taken into consideration when drawing up a plan for the whole garden. It is also important to determine what type of hedging, if any, will suit the area best and can be kept under control easily, thus causing the least annoyance for the neighbours by not shading their plants more than necessary.

The value of space in the garden is important, especially where children are concerned, and a small play area may need to be fitted in for them, particularly when they are young and active. Children can be very hard on a garden and if you can concentrate their activities in one place, the rest of the garden will benefit.

A sand area is cheap, continuously fascinating and easy to pave over later on. Such an area might be planted up, or simply used as an extension to a lawn. Decide on the main structure of your garden first, on the basis of where the sunniest area is. If you wish to grow vegetables they need the sun's energy.

What time of the day will you like to sit out in the garden? Make sure your sitting area receives the sun at this time.

Find the prevailing wind direction and note any unattractive views – you can provide shelter and screening with fencing, which can be clothed in climbing plants or have hedges or shrubs against it.

If you need to separate the productive from amenity part this can be achieved with a hedge or pergola or a line of fruit bushes.

When you take on a new house and garden, then the logical step would be to put ideas down on paper and draw up a plan. Analyse your site, note the orientation of the sun, the direction of the prevailing winds, slopes, views, overlooked areas and any other points which may affect your garden. Then put in:
1. shade and shelter patterns;
2. the exact location for the raised garden beds for vegetables, etc.;
3. the location of an 'outdoor room' as determined by its relation to living room, kitchen and sun;
4. the size and shape of the lawn.

The all-important factor of cost needs to be considered, and a decision made on which item to deal with first. Time of year and weather conditions will influence this, but apart from these considerations the most logical sequence would be as follows:
1. pave the 'outdoor room'
2. plant a hedge
3. prepare the area for vegetables and soft fruit
4. clear and lay turves or sow seed for a lawn
5. plant trees and shrubs, etc.

The above list of jobs to do and their order has simply been suggested as a possible guideline for someone who has never undertaken a new garden before.

Lawns

Just about every garden has a lawn. Such an area of mown grass helps to provide a restful atmosphere to any garden. There is no doubt that a well-cared-for lawn greatly improves the appearance of a garden. For the very tiny garden which may be less than 25 square yards (20 sq m) a chamomile lawn could be the answer and the best variety for use for this purpose is a hybrid of Roman chamomile, called 'Treneague' (mentioned in Chapter 10). This hybrid does not produce any flowers and is low and creeping in habit, so no mowing is needed. The common chamomile (*Anthemis nobilis*) can also be planted out and allowed to spread but this produces single white flowers and grows to about 8 inches (20 cm), and would need cutting to prevent flower-heads appearing, but this would only be once or twice a year. A chamomile lawn has a further advantage in that it withstands dry weather better than the conventional grass lawn.

The Layout of the Lawn in a New Garden

The general shape, size and contours required will need to be decided at an early stage, bearing in mind that about 6 inches (15 cm) of topsoil should remain overall on completion with gradients designed to allow easy mowing in more than one direction and to enable surface water to escape, without collecting into any depressions (hollows). The nature of the actual site – its contours, shape and features such as levels of paths, doors, paved areas or even existing trees – determines the actual form of the new lawn. Generally, simple contours and shapes with no awkward corners or mounds are the most satisfactory and these can often be

made with little movement of soil (earth). With a very large expanse of lawn gentle undulations give interest, but with a very small lawn it is probably better to have either a very slight gentle slope or a level lawn, as this will make the job of mowing that much more straightforward.

Clearing the Area for a Lawn

The first step is to remove all debris, stones, bricks, etc., which the builder may have left on site. Then clear any weeds by following the directions explained in Chapter 3, using the boards and the fork to lever out deep-rooted weeds, etc. It is best to pick a fairly dryish day for this job, if possible. The time of year will no doubt determine when one can actually begin the job of clearing the ground whether for the lawn or borders and garden beds.

After the ground has been cleaned properly, try and leave it for a few weeks in order to allow weeds to germinate and grow again, and then remove them. Then begin the job of raking the soil over, and removing any small stones, etc. Whether the lawn is to be established from turves or seed, the final preparations are similar in order to achieve a firm, fine soil bed area. Generally a better tilth is required for seeding than for turfing down.

A New Lawn Using Turf

The major gain from having the area turfed is that of time, since the turf can be laid in the autumn when seeding may be too late. Turf laid in the spring does run the risk of drying out and not establishing satisfactorily, but this can usually be overcome with the use of a sprinkler. It is important to ensure that when buying turf, it is from a soil of a sandy loam nature and free of stones. The turf should be in a mown condition, and there should be sufficient fibre to hold the turf together.

Good-quality turf should be mainly composed of fine bent and/or fescue grasses and weeds should be absent too. Turf is usually delivered in either 1 foot (30 cm) squares or in rectangular pieces 3 feet by 1 foot (90 by 30 cm), and cut to a uniform thickness, usually 1½ inches (4 cm). Endeavour to carry out the job of turfing when the soil is reasonably dry, to avoid damage to the prepared area. A dryish day will help because boards can then be used.

On some sites it is convenient to lay a single line of turf round the perimeter of the site, then lay the remainder across the site in a forward direction, working to face the unturfed part, which should be maintained in its prepared condition. Lay the turf in broken joints rather like bricks in a wall. Lay each turf flat and tight up to each other. Should any turf seem to be either low or high, adjustment should be made in the soil below, rather than beating the turf down. After the turf is laid, carefully use a light roller over the whole turfed area and then brush in a mixture of fine compost and sand and apply at roughly 5 lb a square yard (say 3 kg per sq m).

See that the turf does not dry out, and if laid in October then apply diluted seaweed solution at the rate of 2 gallons (9 l) to every 10 square yards (8.3 sq m). Apply this after rain has fallen or after watering the area.

A New Lawn from Seed

Generally the best time for sowing grass seed to make a new lawn is during September, but in some mild areas it is worth a gamble to sow in October. A spring sowing is not ruled out entirely but there is a greater risk of drought conditions, which often occur in May. For a first-class lawn it pays to have a seed mixture which contains Chewings fescue and browntop. Avoid mixtures containing rye-grass unless the wear and tear on the lawn is to be exceptional. The rate for sowing is 1½ oz per square yard (42 gm per sq m).

Do this on a dry, clean, raked surface. It is best to divide the seed into two amounts for sowing in transverse directions. Lightly rake the seed in with a spring rake using a scratching motion and try not to cover the seed too deeply. When the grass is showing through give a very light rolling (if possible with a wooden roller); this is to tighten up the soil round the grass roots in readiness for the first mowing. The sown area will very likely need to be protected from bird damage and if the lawn is only modest in size then black cotton can be stretched across supported by sticks.

New-sown lawns should not be mown until the grass is at least 2 inches (5 cm) high, and then it should be carefully topped, preferably using a side wheel mower with sharp blades. Before mowing, collect any stones off the surface. Any coarse grasses or weeds which appear in the new sward should be removed by hand, but later mowings will prevent annual weeds from spreading. A lawn sown at the end of the summer will not need feeding, but the following spring, water in a diluted seaweed solution at the same rate as for the turfed areas.

It needs to be remembered that a regular supply of grass mowings are useful for the compost heap, but if an established lawn has been treated with weedkiller then the first mowings following the application must not be composted. However, it may be safe to compost the second lot of mowings.

Trees for the Garden

For a small or medium-sized garden and particularly in many suburban areas care needs to be taken choosing trees, as they will ultimately be the largest element.

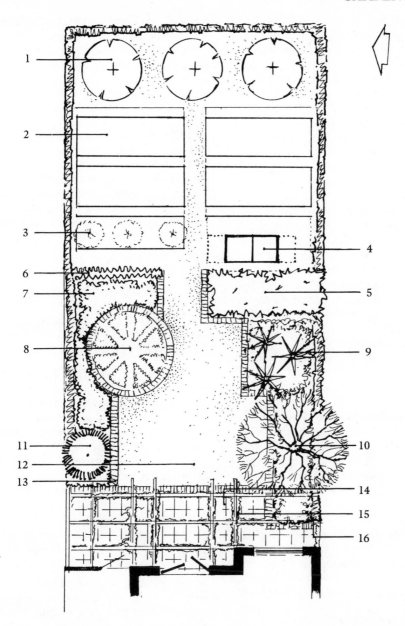

Picture 25 **Garden plan**
Key: 1 fruit trees in grass; 2 raised no digging beds for salads and vegetables; 3 soft fruit
bushes; 4 twin compost bin; 5 flowering evergreen shrubs; 6 climbing plants; 7 low
ground cover plants; 8 herbs; 9 yuccas and low ground cover plants; 10 ornamental tree,
underplanted with bulbs; 11 specimen conifer tree; 12 lawn; 13 brick edging; 14 paved
patio; 15 climbing plants on a pergola; 16 evergreen hedging.

Therefore, before selecting a tree, whether for planting in the border or as a specimen, it is important to be sure of its eventual height, spread, shape and colour. (Tree shapes can be pendulous, pyramidal, horizontal, broad-headed, round-topped or fastigiate.)

The majority of garden centres have a very wide selection of trees and shrubs from which to choose, and at tree nurseries there is an even greater selection, including forest type trees, but never plant ash, oak, beech, sycamore, horse chestnut or any other potential giant in a garden, except in grounds at least an acre (0.4 ha) in extent, and never anywhere near a house under any circumstance.

With the wide range of tree available today to suit most gardens, the following short list should be useful, although the final choice naturally depends on personal preference.

Prunus

One of the most popular type of trees seen at a garden centre is the *Prunus* – commonly referred to as the flowering cherry. The deciduous members of this large genus also include the plum, almond and peach. They are hardy and do well in most types of soil, and prefer being in full sun.

There is no doubt that those which flower in the spring are the best liked, as the masses of pink or white blossom are a glorious sight although a somewhat short-lived one, as flowering is only over a two- or three-week period, and for the remainder of the year – apart from the autumn leaf colour, the tree is nothing very much to look at. There are a number of the Japanese flowering cherries suitable for the garden which come under the heading of *Prunus serrulata*. A few are suggested below.

Prunus serrulata 'Shimidsu Sakura'. One of the loveliest of Japanese cherries with pale pink buds which open to dainty white double flowers 2 inches (5 cm) across in mid-May. The tree grows to a height of 15 feet (4.6 m) and has a spreading habit.

Prunus serrulata 'Amanogawa'. This is a very well-known flowering cherry, and being upright and slim it is a cherry on its own, perhaps as a specimen in the lawn. The flowers are scented semi-double soft pink and clustered at the tips of the branches. Somewhat late-flowering. Height 15 feet (4.6 m) by 3 feet (90 cm).

Prunus serrulata 'Kiku Shidare Zakura' (Cheal's 'Weeping Cherry'). A small tree with arching or drooping branches which are clothed with clusters of pink buds, then double bright pink flowers in mid-May. The foliage is glossy.

Any tree which flowers in late autumn or winter is worth considering and *Prunus subhirtella* 'Autumnalis' does just that. It produces semi-double, white flowers, intermittently from November to March.

With so many varieties of Prunus available, it is important to choose carefully and ascertain the eventual height and spread of any tree before buying.

Betula

Another favourite is the birch (*Betula*). Most birch trees grow anywhere but they are not the easiest of trees to transplant, so it is best to buy one on the small side as once established it will soon grow away.

Betula costata. A very fine tree eventually reaching a height of 20 feet (6 m). The stripped peeling bark is white during the summer and orange in the winter, with rich yellow leaves in the autumn.

Betula pendula 'Youngii'. This is a most graceful weeping small tree and admirably suited to being planted in the lawn. It is dome-shaped and the slender branches reach down to the ground. Height 12 to 15 feet (3.7 to 4.6 m) if trained when young.

Acers

There are a number of Acers (maples) with an elegant form and habit which are ideal for the small to medium-sized garden.

Acer griseum. This is the 'paper-bark maple'. In autumn it has gloriously coloured scarlet leaves and the old bark peels off to reveal new cinnamon coloured bark underneath. Extremely attractive when planted against a background of evergreen trees. Best planted in partial shade in a sheltered position, if possible. Height 12 to 15 feet (3.7 m to 4.6 m).

Acer negundo 'Variegatum'. A very hardy tree with decorative leaves broadly margined cream. Can reach a height of about 20 feet (6 m), so more suitable for a medium or large garden.

Acer ginnala. Can be grown as a bush or small tree, with a height and spread of around 20 feet (6 m). One of the best for autumn colour, leaves turning a fiery red.

Japanese Maples *(Acer palmatum)*

The Japanese maples are small, bushy trees, nearly all slow-growing and ideal for the small garden, making an excellent single specimen or planted in a group to provide brilliant autumn colouring.

There are many varieties and the following are among the most popular.

Acer palmatum. This is the type from which many forms and varieties have originated (mainly the smaller and slower-growing ones). It rapidly attains the size of a low-spreading tree, valued for the orange and red autumnal hues. Height and spread 15 to 20 feet (4.6 to 6 m). Suitable for a medium or large garden.

Acer palmatum 'Dissectum'. Mushroom-shaped when young, ultimately a dense rounded bush. Its deeply lobed finely toothed green leaves turn orange to red in the autumn. Extremely attractive and ideal for the smaller to medium-sized garden. Height and spread 6 to 10 feet (1.83 to 3 m).

Acer palmatum 'Dissectum Atropurpureum'. A similar variety to the above but the leaves are dark red during the summer. Without a doubt one of the best for a small garden, particularly in association with azaleas and heathers (see plate 8(b)). Height and spread around 6 feet (1.8 m), but in some situations may only grow to about 4 feet (1.2 m).

Malus

Deciduous ornamental trees and shrubs. The crab apple, like the ordinary apple, produces beautiful flowers and attractive fruits. The very small apples make excellent jelly. For best results plant in a sunny spot.

Malus 'Floribunda'. The popular 'Japanese Crab', an exceptionally beautiful semi-pendulous tree with arching branches smothered in masses of bright red buds which open to palest pink or white flowers. Makes an ideal specimen tree in the lawn. The height can vary from 6 feet (1.83 m) to about 12 feet (3.7 m). Pruning consists of thinning out branches every few years.

Malus pumila 'John Downie'. One of the best-fruiting crabs with fruit of ovate shape bright yellow and red. Useful as a pollinator apple.

Corylus

Deciduous and attractive nut-bearing trees and shrubs with male flowers in catkins, hazels produce useful amounts of nuts providing the early flowers escape frost damage and there are a number of ornamental forms for use in the garden.

Corylus avellana 'Aurea' This is the soft yellow-leaved form of the native 'cobnut' which grows 12 to 20 feet in height (3.7 m to 6 m). A good one to have in a 'wild' part of a garden.

Corylus avellana 'Contorta'. Known as the 'Corkscrew Hazel' with curiously twisted branches. Slow growing to about 8 to 10 feet (2.4 m to 3 m) in height. An attractive winter feature when in catkin.

Robinia pseudoacacia 'Frisia' (see plate 7)

A very lovely tree with leaves a rich golden yellow from spring to autumn. Height to about 18 to 20 feet (5.5 m to 6 m). Needs a stout supporting stake for a few years.

Conifers

In many gardens where there is some space available, and this more often than not is the lawn, then a well positioned conifer can be an interesting focal point, or form a striking contrast planted among low-growing azaleas and heathers. Most garden centres have a bewildering assortment of all types of conifers and choosing the right one for your garden is not always that easy. With many more small gardens than ever before it is even more important to select one which will give character and

atmosphere to any garden.

So the following selection will hopefully make your final choice that much easier. However, do make sure it is correctly named and check with the nursery or garden centre as to the ultimate height and spread.

Chamaecyparis lawsoniana 'Columnaris Glauca'. This makes a lovely specimen being narrow, erect and tall with blue foliage. Height and spread 12 feet by 4 feet (3.7 m by 1.2 m).

Chamaecyparis lawsoniana 'Stewartii'. A handsome and more conically shaped specimen with soft gold foliage. Height and spread 10 feet by 4 feet (3 m by 1.2 m).

Chamaecyparis lawsoniana 'Lanei Aurea'. Another lovely one with golden foliage, but more compact than 'Stewartii'. Height and spread 8 feet by 4 feet (2.4 m by 1.2 m).

Chamaecyparis lawsoniana 'Eliwoodii'. A charming, slow-growing variety with erect branches densely covered with feathery glaucous-blue foliage. Excellent for a small garden. Height and spread 9 feet by 5 feet (2.7 m by 1.5 m).

Juniperus (Cupressaceae).
This is another large genus containing many varied forms which include:

Juniperus communis 'Hibernica' (Irish Juniper). This makes a dense pillar of deep green foliage. Ideal for a small garden. Will eventually reach a height and spread of 10 feet by 2 feet (3 m by 60 cm).

Juniperus virginiana 'Skyrocket'. A most effective and extremely narrow columnar tree with blue-green foliage. Ideal with heathers. Height and spread 8 feet by 9 inches to 15 inches (2.4 m by 23 cm to 38 cm).

When planting conifers, it is important to water the soil and foliage copiously, and continue to do this during any dry spell until they are established.

Hedging
A good hedge properly maintained will provide a very efficient and relatively inexpensive form of protection.

The majority of new homes will most likely have a post and wire or close board fence as a boundary to the garden, but while these types of fencing may be effective as a boundary partition they do not have the aesthetic appeal of a hedge. Virtually all hedging requires clipping to maintain a reasonable shape and size, but there are some kinds which only need to be pruned rather than clipped or trimmed. For small- to medium-sized gardens it is a matter of whether the hedge has been chosen for its colourful foliage – these generally make formal hedges and are trimmed with shears – or for its flowers – a flowering hedge would be pruned using secateurs.

It is best to select plants to make a hedge which will be strong and dense to the ground level, and attain a height of between 3 and 6 feet (90 cm and 1.83 m), especially when one has to consider one's neighbour because of possible shadows being cast onto certain plants or shrubs which dislike being in the shade or partial shade. However, most hedges can be restrained and therefore kept in bounds without too much trouble.

Some of the popular formal hedges are listed here:

Foliage Hedges
Fagus sylvatica (Common Beech). Very useful in lime soils and makes an excellent hedge. The brown leaves persist through the winter. Best to avoid heavy wet soils. Will reach a height of about 5 feet (1.5 m) in five years.

It is important to cut the side growth back in late August or early spring and leave the leading shoots to grow to the desired height. Plant 2 feet (60 cm) apart.

Carpinus betulus. This is easier to establish on the heavier types of soils than beech. Plant 2 feet (60 cm) apart, and prune as for beech.

Crataegus monogyna. The common species of the native 'Hawthorn', 'Quick' or 'May'. This can be planted on its own or mixed with beech or hornbeam. Makes an excellent hedge. Plant 1½ feet (45 cm) apart. Best for medium to large gardens.

The privet 'Ligustrum' is not really recommended as it robs the soil so badly and is very dull in colour.

Flowering and Foliage Hedges
Most of these are more or less informal.

Berberis thunbergii. The foliage is brilliantly coloured in the spring and autumn. Plant 2 feet (60 cm) apart. Trim in the winter. Height 4 to 6 feet (1.22 to 1.83 m).

Berberis thunbergii 'Erecta'. Has stiff vertical habit, making a good narrow hedge. Plant 1½ feet (45 cm) apart. Height 2 to 4 feet (60 cm to 1.2 m).

Cotoneaster simonsii. A well-known semi-evergreen, erect growing shrub, with red berries. Plant 2 feet (60 cm) apart in October to March. Trim in the winter. Eventual height 6 to 8 feet (1.83 to 2.44 m).

Lonicera nitida fertilis. For hedging this is an improvement on nitida. The small box-like, glossy leaves densely crowd the erect branches. Must be pruned hard otherwise the black berries are freely produced. Plant 1 foot (30 cm) apart. Height 4 to 6 feet (1.2 m to 1.83 m).

Flowering and Berrying Hedges

These are, in the main, informal, and due allowance needs to be made for them to spread; 3 feet (90 cm), is the minimum width that ought to be allowed.

Berberis darwinii. An evergreen with rich orange-yellow flowers in April and May. Bluish-purple berries. Plant 2 feet (60 cm) apart from October to March, and prune after flowering. Height 4 to 6 feet (1.2 to 1.83 m).

Escallonia

These are hardy and half-hardy evergreen and deciduous.

Escallonia macrantha or *Escallonia ingramii.* Make excellent hedges, especially in coastal areas. Plant 2 feet (60 cm) apart in September or during March/April. Trim after flowering in late summer. Height 4 to 6 feet (1.2 to 1.83 m).

Escallonia 'C. F. Ball'. Another excellent one for a hedge. Has large deep red flowers. Prune after flowering to encourage a second flush of flowers. Prune lightly in the spring. Plant 2 feet (60 cm) apart. Height 4 to 6 feet (1.2 to 1.83 m).

Olearia haastii. An evergreen with greyish oval leaves. Daisy-like flowers from July onwards. Plant 3 feet (90 cm) apart; prune lightly after flowering. Height about 4 feet (1.2 m).

Pyracantha rogersiana. Evergreen with white flowers followed by masses of red berries. Makes an excellent hedge. Plant

2½ feet (75 cm) apart; prune lightly in the spring and if need be in the summer. Height 4 to 6 feet (1.2 to 1.83 m).

Coniferous Hedges

Those listed below will form dense evergreen formal hedges.

Chamaecyparis lawsoniana. One of the most popular of hedges, and equally suitable as a wind screen. It is better to plant the variety named *Chamaecyparis lawsoniana* 'Alumii', which has bluish-grey and sea-green foliage. Plant 2 to 2½ feet (60 cm to 75 cm) apart. Height about 8 feet (2.4 m).

Chamaecyparis lawsoniana 'Fletcheri'. This has bluish-grey feathery foliage. Plant 2 feet (60 cm) apart. Height 4 to 6 feet (1.2 to 1.83 m).

Taxus baccata (Common Yew). This makes a wonderful hedge, and is not so slow-growing as is generally believed. Plant in September or early October or late March/April. Plant 1½ to 2 feet (45 to 60 cm) apart, and trim in late summer and taper the hedge towards the top. Height 5 to 6 feet (1.52 m to 1.83 m). *Caution:* all yews are highly poisonous to livestock.

Low-growing Hedges

These normally do not exceed 3 to 4 feet (90 cm to 1.2 m) in height.

Berberis verruculosa. This is an evergreen with dense glossy green foliage. Pendant golden flowers in May with handsome fruit. Plant at 2 feet (60 cm) apart from October to March. It is important to prune after flowering. Height 3 to 4 feet (90 cm to 1.2 m).

Lavandula spica (Old English). This has long spikes of pale greyish-blue flowers. Must be trimmed after flowering and shaped in April. Plant 1 foot (30 cm) apart. Height 3 to 4 feet (90 cm to 1.2 m).

Plate 7   Early spring in the garden

Plate 8 (*a*) The striking flowers of the Clematis 'Nelly Moser'

(*b*) Japanese Maple, Azalea and Heathers complement each other in this arrangement

Lavandula spica 'Nana Munstead Dwarf. Has dark lavender-blue flowers. Plant 15 inches (38 cm) apart. Trim in April. Height 1 foot (30 cm). More suitable as an edging within the garden itself, rather than as a boundary hedge.

Hebe anomala. Erect, evergreen and compact with white flowers in July and August. Plant 1½ feet (45 cm) apart; trim and shape in the spring. Height about 2 feet (60 cm).

Prunus cistena. An ideal low hedge with single white flowers and deep crimson foliage. Plant 2 feet (60 cm) apart. Restrict annual increase in height to 6 inches (15 cm). Trim after flowering. Any height up to 4 to 5 feet (1.2 to 1.52 m).

Shrubs and Ground Cover

Many people want a garden filled with attractive and colourful shrubs. With the limited space in this book it is not possible to describe all the many hundreds of shrubs and ground cover plants available today. Instead, a small selection noted for their foliage and flowers and in some cases their fragrance are listed.

The actual scale of planting shrubs will to a large extent depend on the size of garden, and the type of soil. There may be a situation where just one decorative shrub could be a feature, but generally it is better to group shrubs simply and boldly.

Should the garden be protected by some hedging whether evergreen or deciduous then this could be a useful backcloth to set off the form and beauty of many kinds of shrubs.

Fragrant shrubs in the list are identified by an asterisk (*). Shrubs and ground cover are listed in alphabetical order.

Shrubs

Acer palmatum, Acer palmatum 'Dissectum' and *Acer p. 'Dissectum Atropurpureum'* are listed elsewhere in this chapter under trees. In some catalogues they may be classified as shrubs.

Arundinaria. Many of the most extensively planted 'bamboos' are known by this familiar name, but the majority are included under various other genera.

Arundinaria murielae. Forms clumps of slender arching canes 8 to 12 feet (2.4 m to 3.7 m) high bearing elegant plumes of soft green foliage.

Arundinaria nitida. An ideal hardy 'bamboo' for the small garden. It does well in the semi-shade, and succeeds in most types of soil, even better in moist soil. This beautiful species differs from *A. murielae* in having purple-tinged canes and smaller leaves. In the first year the canes are leafless. Best to plant in April/May. Old worn-out canes should be cut right out in April. Height 8 to 10 feet (2.4 to 3.5 m).

Azaleas

These are a series of rhododendron, and fall into the two groups, evergreen and deciduous. The evergreens are dwarf and the deciduous are taller and broader. Better to refer to a reliable nursery catalogue as for rhododendrons, as so many are available. The deciduous varieties provide colourful flowers in the spring and in autumn the leaves assume rich hues. The evergreen ones are Japanese; all are low-growing and somewhat spreading. They usually flower in May/June. A soil free of lime is required, and partial shade is preferred. Use leaf-mould or tree-leaf compost mixed with peat when planting.

Berberis

This is a large and fascinating group of

both decidiuous and evergreen shrubs, and fairly easy to cultivate. The deciduous varieties need to be in the sun but the evergreens will grow quite well in shade.

Recommended are the following:

Berberis darwinii. Noted for its small holly-like leaves with masses of yellow flowers in the spring – usually in April and May. Grows to 6 to 8 feet (1.83 m to 2.4 m). Will tolerate salt-laden winds.

Berberis linerfolia 'Orange King'. A beautiful shrub with deep orange flowers turning to red in April. Has long glossy leaves. Berries are purple. Height about 6 feet (1.83 m) with a spread of 4 feet (1.2 m).

Berberis stenophylla. This forms a dense shrub with long arching branches clothed in orange flowers. A hardy type but needs plenty of space as it grows to about 10 feet (3 m) in height and spread.

Deciduous varieties of Berberis:

Berberis thunbergii. A bushy and very lovely shrub with flowers in the spring of a straw colour suffused red, and again in the autumn with bright-red fruit and foliage. A good hedging subject too. Height about 4 to 6 feet (1.2 m to 1.83 m), spread about 4 feet (1.2 m).

Berberis wilsonae. A small-growing but graceful variety with bright-yellow flowers in July, with coral berries and autumn tints. One of the best for summer and autumn effect, particularly when massed in front of border. Height 3 to 4 feet (90 cm to 1.2 m) and a spread of 6 feet (1.83 m).

*Buddleia

The buddleias are vigorous shrubs and thrive in most soils. Butterflies are attracted to the sweetly scented flowers.

Rapid grower. The following two are recommended:

Buddleia davidii. One of the best-known of the Buddleias, having dark lavender flowers from July to September. It is important to cut back drastically last season's shoots to within a few inches of old wood in February. Can grow to 12 feet (3.7 m) so needs to be carefully sited. Plant in the autumn or late March.

Buddleia fallowiana 'Alba'. This shrub has very sweetly scented white flowers with an orange eye, flowering in July and August. Needs to be planted in a more sheltered position afforded by other shrubs or near a wall. Height eventually 8 feet (2.4 m).

*Choisya ternata

A splendid evergreen shrub often referred to as the 'Mexican Orange Blossom'. Bears fragrant star-like flowers in May, and spasmodically during late summer and autumn. Forms a rounded bush with glossy foliage. Does best in a sheltered spot as it is slightly tender. It is best to prune after flowering by simply shortening the straggling shoots. Height and spread 6 feet (1.83 m).

Cornus (Dogwood)

The following are recommended. They are deciduous shrubby varieties grown for winter wood and foliage effect.

Cornus alba sibirica 'Westonbirt'. An excellent and effective shrub with sealing-wax-red bark. The foliage is a pleasing fresh green; berries are steel blue. Height and spread 6 feet (1.83 m).

Cornus alba 'Spaethii'. A variegated foliage shrub, it retains the golden colour throughout the season. The red bark is outstanding in winter. Height and spread around 6 feet (1.83 m).

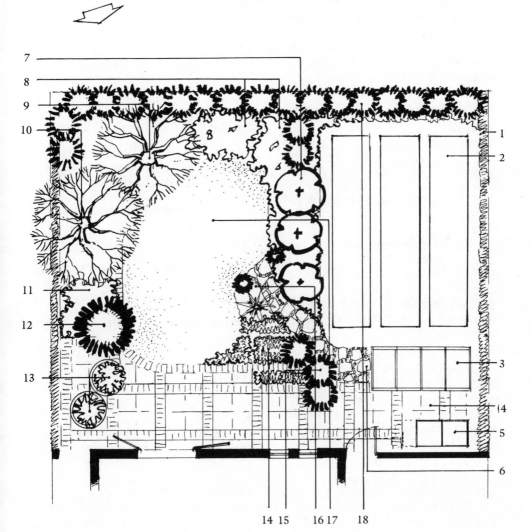

Picture 26 **Garden plan**
Key: 1 evergreen hedge; 2 no digging beds for salads and vegetables; 3 dutch light cold frame;
    4 patio constructed of paving and bricks; 5 twin compost bin; 6 stone and gravel path;
    7 fruit tree; 8 mixed low ground cover and flowering shrubs; 9 deciduous ornamental tree;
    10 specimen tree; 11 low ground cover plants; 12 specimen conifer tree; 13 plants in
    containers; 14 mixed herbs; 15 narrow conifer trees; 16 shrubs and columnar conifer tree;
    17 lawn; 18 screen planting of conifer trees.

Cornus stolonifera 'Flaviramea'. This yellow-stemmed dogwood provides a natural contrast to the red stems of the preceding variety. The leaves are a soft green in summer but turn a pale clear yellow before falling and revealing the yellow bark. This is one which ought to be planted in association with evergreen shrubs. Height 6 feet (1.83 m) and spread between 6 and 8 feet (1.83 and 2.44 m).

Cornus kousa. A tall, elegant Japanese shrub with white bracts poised on slender erect stalks on the horizontal branches. Colours well in the autumn. Height some 15 to 20 feet (4.6 to 6 m).

Cotoneasters

The Cotoneasters along with the Berberis are among the most useful of shrubs. They will succeed in virtually any situation, even a cold sunless one. They will produce masses of berries in the autumn even if their flowers are not the primary consideration.

Cotoneaster franchetti. A semi-evergreen shrub with sage green leaves which have a silvery tint. The slender arching branches are covered with orange-red berries in the autumn. Tall-growing, reaching a height of 10 feet (3 m) and a spread of 6 feet (1.83 m).

Cotoneaster bullata. One of the best of the taller forms with long arching branches with large corrugated shaped leaves which colour in the autumn. A good one to form part of a group, it appreciates the sun and requires good light conditions if it is to bear red berries in large numbers. Height 6 to 8 feet (1.83 m to 2.44 m) by 5 feet (1.52 m).

Cotoneaster conspicua. A low-growing type with masses of orange-red berries. Graceful with arching branches usually not more than 4 to 5 feet high (1.22 to 1.52 m) but wide spreading. Flowers white, covering the plant in early summer.

Cytisus (Brooms)

Free-flowering shrubs with yellow pea-shaped flowers in the spring.

Cytisus praecox. One of the most graceful free-flowering kinds, with a flowering period from April to June. Height and spread between 3 and 4 feet (90 cm and 1.22 m).

Cytisus albus. Known as the 'White Portugal Brown'. Fairly compact bush with white flowers in May. Height up to 10 feet (3 m) and spread of 8 feet (2.44 m).

Forsythia

A very beautiful early-spring flowering shrub. Of open habit and well worth planting, even in exposed places.

Forsythia ovata. A dwarf and bushy variety flowering very early in the spring, February to March. Height 4 feet (1.22 m) and spread of 3 feet (90 cm).

Forsythia 'Beatrix Farrand'. Makes a lovely symmetrical bush, smothered in deep golden yellow flowers in spring. Height up to 8 feet (2.4 m) and spread of 5 feet (1.5 m) after ten years.

Fuchsia

The well-known shrub flowering between June and October. Frequently found in mild coastal areas. They can be grown successfully in less favourable locations provided they can be protected in some way during the winter.

Fuchsia gracilis. An elegant shrub with small red and purple flowers and small leaves. Fairly hardy. Height 4 to 6 feet (1.22 to 1.83 m) and spread of 6 feet (1.83 m).

Fuchsia 'Madame Cornellison'. A dwarf variety with large semi-double flowers, reflexed sepals with white corolla, continuing to flower well into October. Height 2 to 3 feet (60 cm to 90 cm) and a spread of 4 feet (1.22 m).

Fuchsia magellanica 'Riccartonii'. One of the hardiest. The scarlet and purple flowers are freely produced on vigorous branch growths. Height and spread 6 feet (1.83 m).

Hamamelis (Witch Hazel)
A beautiful winter-flowering shrub or small tree, blooming on leafless branches from December to March. It is immune to frost and the hazel-like foliage frequently gives good autumn colour. Useful in association with *Erica carnea* varieties.

Hamamelis mollis. A unique shrub flowering from January to March. The scented yellow flowers are very distinct and are followed by grey leaves. An extremely useful winter flowering shrub, is hardy, but requires a good soil to thrive well. Height and spread 7 to 8 feet (2.13 m to 2.44 m), but is wider at the top than the base.

Hebe
Often referred to as 'veronicas', they are excellent evergreen shrubs and well-suited to most gardens. Suggested varieties include:

Hebe 'Autumn Glory'. A hardy broad-leaved variety with large bluish-mauve flowers which are freely produced from August until well into October. One of the best sorts. Height 3 feet (90 cm).

Hebe brachysiphon. This is probably the most widely planted hebe, and makes a fine specimen well clothed to the ground. White flowers on short spikes are freely produced from June onwards.

Height and spread about 4 to 5 feet (1.22 to 1.52 m).

Hypericum
The shrubby 'St John's Wort' will thrive in almost any well-drained soil. They are desirable summer and autmun flowering shrubs. There are deciduous and evergreen sorts. The deciduous species are usually small bushy upright shrubs. They are useful for ground cover but a few such as 'Hidcote' can form an attractive low hedge.

Hypericum patulum henryi. One of the best sorts with large flowers which are late in blooming. Rich bronze seed pods and crimson red foliage in the autumn. Height 4 feet (1.22 m) and spread of 3 feet (90 cm). Semi-evergreen.

Hypericum p. 'Hidcote'. One of the largest flowered of the hardy species. Saucer-shaped flower. Classed as semi-evergreen but in mild areas will come through well. Height 5 feet (1.52 m) by 4 feet (1.22 m).

Hypericum 'Rowallene Hybrid'. A very fine plant but needs a sheltered site. Has rich golden-yellow flowers from July and keeps on flowering until the frosts. Suitable too for walls. Height 5 feet (1.52 m) by 3 feet (90 cm).

Lavandula
Lavenders have been described already: see pages 68–69. They make excellent low-growing shrubs and hedges.

Myrtus
The 'Myrtles' are an easily cultivated and effective family of white-flowered fragrant evergreens for the milder areas.

Myrtus communis (The Common Myrtle). A very attractive shrub or small tree, with small, glossy leaves which are aromatic when crushed. The white flowers are borne profusely in July. Attains a height of 10 feet (3 m) and a spread of 8 feet (2.44 m). Does well against a wall.

Myrtus communis 'Tarentina'. A very pretty compact, small-leaved variety, which flowers freely. A little gem. Height 3 to 4 feet (90 cm to 1.22 m) by 2 feet (60 cm).

Philadelphus (Mock Orange)

This shrub is often incorrectly called *Syringa*, which is, in fact, the botanical name for lilac. It is renowned for the scent of the flowers, which are mainly white and adorn their arching branches in June/July. The variety 'Norma' is nearly scentless. They will grow even in the poorest of soils, but really need mulching with leaf-mould or tree-leaf compost, and feeding at intervals with liquid seaweed solution. They need to be pruned after flowering, cutting back the young vigorous growths on the main stems. Also some thinning is advised.

Philadelphus 'Beauclerk'. A splendid hybrid, with broad-petalled flowers 2½ inches (6 cm) across. Sweetly scented. height and spread about 6 feet (1.83 m).

Philadelphus 'Virginal'. Still one of the best double white flowering kinds. Enormous panicles of semi-double pure-white strongly scented flowers. Can attain a height of 10 feet (3 m) by 5 feet (1.52 m).

Philadelphus 'Manteau d'Hermine'. Exceptionally free-flowering with double creamy-white vanilla-scented flowers. Height 3 feet (90 cm) by 4 feet (1.22 m).

Potentilla

A deciduous low-growing shrub which is hardy and accommodating, but prefers a moderately moist soil. The rose-like flowers appear from June to September.

Potentilla fruticosa 'Abbotswood'. Forms a bush with yellow flowers and the grey-green foliage makes this a distinct form. Height 3 feet (90 cm) spread 5 feet (1.52 m).

Potentilla fruticosa grandiflora 'Jackman's variety'. This has large yellow flowers with deeply lobed foliage. Height and spread 4 feet (1.22 m).

Potentilla fruticosa 'Tangerine'. A bush of shapely habit. In hot weather the flowers are bright yellow, but in cool weather the scarlet buds open tangerine orange. Height 2 feet (61.5 cm) and spread 4 feet (1.22 m).

Rhododendron

Of the many species, hybrids, early and late varieties, of the dwarf kinds it is better to refer to any nursery catalogue. The common mauve species is *R. ponticum*, but hybrid seedlings in assorted colours as supplied by most nurseries are perfectly satisfactory.

They thrive in peat soils although this is not essential. They do fairly well on moist non-chalky soils, and the addition of leaf-mould is advised when planting. Generally very hot situations do not suit them and light shade is beneficial.

Roses

The rose is without a doubt one of the most popular of flowering shrubs and is a firm favourite for those who enjoy both colour and fragrance. However, to do justice to this vast genus would require a volume to itself. Once the main structure planting has been carried out then the reader can decide whether or not to include a rose or two.

Certainly a climbing rose could adorn a wall within view of the house, and a few of these roses are recommended in the section under 'Climbing plants'. There is a very wide choice of books on the subject of roses and ample illustrative literature available. On the whole the rose is not very demanding, and will grow in most soils, but the clay-based soils are reckoned to be the best. They do require ample sun to ensure profuse flowering. The ideal time to plant is November, but it can be done from mid-October to the end of December or in March/April.

Carefully remove the top 6 to 9 inches (15 cm to 23 cm) of topsoil and place on one side. Then loosen the lower soil with a fork and work in some sharp gritty sand and a double handful of leaf-mould, tree-leaf compost or semi-mature veganic compost. Instructions about spacing and pruning, etc., are usually supplied with the rose. As for maintenance they will need an annual mulching of leaf-mould, tree-leaf or veganic compost, which could include peat. Also in dry weather see that they receive plenty of water, and give liquid feed of diluted seaweed solution at the rate of 1 gallon (2 l) to each rose bush.

Of the many shrub roses the following are recommended:

*Shrub Roses
These are mainly hybrids and cultivars of the old species.

Rosa × alba. Robust shrubs up to 6 feet (1.83 m) with smooth green wood, and wonderful scented flowers in June and July.

Rosa × alba 'Maiden's Blush'. A small shrub with bluish pink, fading paler, flat, double flowers and grey-green foliage. Height 4 feet (1.22 m).

Rosa × alba 'Celestial'. Has the most exquisite rich pink buds which open to shell-pink double flowers 4 to 5 inches (10 cm to 13 cm) across.

Rosa × Bourboniana 'Kathleen Harrop'. One of the prettiest and constantly in flower with superb scent. They are thornless. Use as a shrub or can be planted as a pillar. Height 5 to 6 feet (1.52 to 1.83 m).

*Modern Hybrid Shrub Roses
This group is best treated as vigorous Floribundas or Hybrid Musks. Prune in February by removing all the old twiggy growth and encourage young basal shoots. Normally June to July flowering.

*'Golden Wings' A gem of a rose. Beautiful soft yellow single flower and well scented. Grows to 5 feet (1.52 m).

*'Nevada'. The almost thornless branches are clothed with masses of pale pink buds opening to semi-double creamy-white flowers 5 inches (12.5 cm) across. A very beautiful sight in May/June/July, again in August and intermittently onwards. Vigorous in habit. Grows to a height of 7 feet (2.13 m).

*'Boule de Neige'. A Bourbon Rose which produces fragrant, creamy-white very full, round flowers continuously from mid-June throughout the summer. Hardy and erect growing, it reaches a height of 5 feet (1.52 m).

*'Tuscany'. This is a Gallica shrub with crimson-purple gold-centred bloom, semi-double and slightly fragrant, appearing in June. Bushy and grows to a height of 4 feet (1.22 m).

*Rosmarinus officinalis
The well-known sweet smelling shrub Rosemary. Has blue flowers in May. Trim to shape and shorten long shoots after flowering. Height 5 feet (1.5 m) and spread of 7 feet (2.13 m). Also refer to Chapter 10.

Spiraea

An extremely free-flowering and easily grown shrub. The individual flowers are small and only last about a month. Spiraeas require careful pruning, and some varieties need to be pruned in the spring after flowering. The summer flowering varieties require fairly hard pruning in February.

Spiraea × arguta. Called 'The Bridal Wreath'. Has stems which are covered in dainty white flowers in April/May. Fresh green leaves all summer. Height 7 feet (2.13 m) and spread 5 feet (1.52 m).

Spiraea thunbergii. This is the earliest to flower – March – and is one of the best. It is semi-dwarf type and does not like a lime soil. Height 4 feet (1.22 m) by 6 feet (1.83 m) spread.

Spiraea bella. Clusters of dainty rose-pink flowers on arching sprays with pointed leaves. Height 6 feet by 4 feet spread (1.83 m by 1.22 m).

Tamarisk

The tamarisks are hardy and deciduous. Will grow in most soils and favour drier soils within range of the sea.

Tamarisk gallica. This is the common tamarisk. It has pink flowers in May and June.

Tamarisk petandra. Pale-pink scented flowers intermingled with glaucous foliage. Both these sorts reach a height of 10 feet (3 m) and have a spread of 7 feet (2.13 m). Tamarisk should be cut back severely after planting, but otherwise no pruning. It can be grown on its own or among low bushes.

Viburnum

These are both deciduous and evergreen flowering shrubs. They are admirable for small gardens. Winter-flowering.

Viburnum × bodnantense. A deciduous shrub with deep pink flower buds which open to fragrant, rose-coloured tubular flowers in rounded clusters over several weeks. Frost resistant. Height 9 feet (2.9 m) with spread of 4 feet (1.22 m).

Viburnum tinus 'Laurustinus'. An evergreen and possibly the easiest to grow. The leaves are of medium size, smooth and dark green. The flower buds are pink and open to form large flat cymes of white flowers from December to April. Height and spread 8 feet to 10 feet (2.4 m to 3 m).

Viburnum henryi. An autumn berrying shrub. A hardy species of value because of its fine show of red berries which later turn black. The evergreen leaves are dark green, smooth and narrow. White flowers in June. Upright habit. Height up to 8 feet (2.4 m).

Viburnum tomentosum 'Lanarth'. Deciduous. A particularly interesting one with tiers of spreading branches which are covered in large clusters of snow-white flowers. The fresh apple-green leaves retain their freshness all summer. Height 8 to 10 feet (2.4 to 3 m) equal spread.

Yucca

A genus of distinctly tropical appearance. Even so they are hardy and will grow anywhere, but prefer lighter shady soils. They have long sword-like leaves and spectacular creamy white pendulous flowers in panicles. Recommended are:

Yucca filamentosa The stem of this is below the ground. The leaves are long and tapering to a point, 2 inches (5 cm) wide and stiff. It flowers in July and August. It is good for either mass planting or as single specimens. Height 4 feet (1.22 m) or more.

Yucca gloriosa. This is a tall thick-stemmed species with stiff, pointed leaves, and flowers from July to September. Height 7 feet to 8 feet (2.13 to 2.4 m).

Ground Cover Plants

The art of successful ground cover planting is to ensure the thorough cleaning of the soil and the choice of plants suited to the overall scheme of the garden. To clean the soil properly follow the board clearing method as described in Chapter 3, making sure that all perennial creeping weeds are removed along with any other extraneous materials. Far better to delay planting of any ground cover plants, before even attempting to plant. Once the plants are established and beginning to spread, any odd weed which comes through can easily be removed. Then it is simply a matter of mulching at intervals and maintaining any plants which need to be trimmed or lightly pruned, as the case may be.

In designing any border, which could be almost virtually labour-saving, it will be appreciated the value of having ground cover not only means a virtual weed suppression and conserving of moisture; they also contribute to the garden scene throughout the year with their foliage, flower and form.

The following are recommended:

Berberis candidula. This is an excellent ground cover, evergreen, dense and spreading. Dark glossy green leaves with silvery underside, bright-yellow flowers April/May and June. Oval purple berries. Height 2 feet (60 cm) with a spread of 3 to 4 feet (90 cm to 1.2 m).

Cotoneaster horizontalis. Deciduous. This is the well-known dwarf spreading variety, suitable for rockeries, walls, banks, and simply to cover the ground. The small red berries are freely pro-duced in the autumn and the small glossy green leaves turn bright orange and red. The height is very rarely above 3 feet (90 cm) and the spread up to 8 feet (2.4 m) or so.

Cotoneaster salicifolius 'Autumn Fire'. A very useful plant with very large leaves – willow-like in shape – and large bright-red berries. Height 1 foot (30 cm); spread up to 12 feet (3.7 m).

Cytisus purpureus incarnatus. This variety has soft-mauve-pink flowers in June/July. Also useful in groups on low walls. Height 2 feet (60 cm) with a spread of 4 feet (1.2 m) or so.

Cytisus × *kewensis.* This spreading plant has pale-yellow flowers in April/May. Height 1½ feet (45 cm) and spread to about 4 feet (1.22 m).

*Daphne cneorum. Evergreen and a great favourite on account of its frag-rant pink flowers in May. Low-spreading and best-suited to rock gar-dens.

Euonymus radicans. A low-growing evergreen ground cover for any site and soil. Height 1 foot (30 cm) with a spread up to 6 feet (1.83 m).

Euonymus r. variegata. A silver variegated form of the above.

Heathers

Heathers are one of the most delightful of ground cover plants, though they are not to everyone's taste. Nevertheless they combine well with dwarf conifers, azaleas and many other shrubs.

The really true heather *Calluna vulgaris* is the familiar common one and can be seen growing on many a moorland, and while this particular one dislikes limy soils as do many of the *Ericas* and *Daboecia,* the *Erica carnea, Erica* × *darlyensis, Erica mediterranea* and *Erica stricta* and their varieties will actually do quite well in a neutral soil.

So even an ordinary garden soil means that many heathers can be grown successfully. By careful selection it is possible to have colour ranging from white through the pinks, purple and deep mauve.

In addition, there is a wide range of foliage colour in the different greens, silvery green, gold and copper, and added to this some species and varieties provide autumnal hues during the winter months.

Many interesting effects can be achieved not only in the rock garden, but as low decorative hedges.

The soil needs to be well cleared of perennial and creeping type weeds, as trying to remove these when the heathers are getting established is extremely difficult. Planting can take place, weather permitting, any time from September to April, but with plants now available in containers the period of the year is not all that critical. Ideally the soil should be moist and warm, conditions which are normal during the autumn and late spring, which would therefore seem the best time. Generally plant them 12 to 15 inches (30 to 38 cm) apart.

When planting, use peat; the quantity will depend on whether the soil is lime-free, and can hold moisture well during hot dry spells in a summer. Where the soil is neutral or very slightly alkaline, then liberal amounts of peat can be incorporated into the soil at the time of planting, and this gives the plants something to root into. Also, mix the peat not only with surrounding soil but put a good double handful into each planting hole. Leaf-mould or tree-leaf compost are both very useful and if mixed with peat can be applied around all heathers. The important factor is, of course, to choose the right species of heather to suit the right type of soil. To achieve the best effects plant

three, five or more of one variety in any one group.

After flowering, trim and shape the heather plants with well-sharpened garden shears.

The following selection can be planted in ordinary, neutral-type garden soil providing peat and/or leaf-mould is incorporated at time of planting.

Erica carnea 'Springwood White'. Bright-green foliage with pure-white flowers. A most attractive plant flowering from late winter and April.

Erica carnea 'Springwood Pink'. Similar to above but foliage is a mid-green with flowers showing white at first, then changing to a clear pink later. Like Springwood White a vigorous grower. Same period of flowering as the white.

Erica carnea 'Vivelli'. Foliage dark green turning to a bronze during the winter. Flowers are carmine red on spikes. An excellent compact grower flowering late winter and through the spring.

Erica carnea 'King George'. Dark-green foliage and flowers are bells of deep rose pink, freely produced. Flowering midwinter to spring.

Erica carnea 'Ruby Glow'. Dark-green foliage with brown buds. Vigorous and spreading. Flowers late winter to spring and flowers are as red as any ruby, as the name suggests.

Erica carnea 'Foxhollow'. Foliage is light, yellow-green, becoming a rich yellow in the winter time. The flowers are white bells on opening, slowly changing to pale pink. A very attractive one noted for its coloured winter foliage, which is late winter to spring. Low-growing and vigorous.

Erica darleyensis 'Arthur Johnson'. Light-green foliage. Flowers are bright mauve-pink in long spikes. Long flowering period during the winter months.

Erica × *darleyensis* 'Furzey'. Foliage is dark green and even darker green over the winter period. Flowers are dark rose/purple long spikes.

Erica × *darleyensis* 'Jack H. Brummage'. Summer foliage is a light yellow, and then turning golden-green and in winter to a clear gold, depending on the situation. Flowers are a deep pink on short spikes.

All the above three varieties of *E.* × *darleyensis* have a long flowering period and are very hardy.

The following selection require a neutral or acid soil to thrive:

Erica cineria (Bell heathers). These prefer a position which is a little on the dry side, and they belong to a group which needs a neutral or acid soil. Best to plant them in full sun and incorporate generous amounts of peat at planting time. All flower from early summer until the autumn.

Erica cineria 'Duncan Fraser'. Deep-green foliage. Flowers white with delicate pink blush. Vigorous and spreading.

Erica cineria 'Eden Valley'. A very pretty heather with light-green foliage. Flowers are bi-colour – each of lilac with a white base. Free-flowering and low and spreading.

Erica vagans. These will tolerate a slightly alkaline environment but still use plenty of peat when planting and mulching. Growth habit is neat and being a rapid grower soon covers a large area. Useful for planting towards the back of a border of heathers. Long-lasting display of flowers during the summer and autumn.

Erica vagans 'Mrs D. F. Maxwell'. Foliage deep glossy green. Flowers are cerise. A neat bushy growth with long spikes.

Erica vagans 'Lyonesse'. Foliage of deep fresh green and white flowers which are long-lasting, from July to October. Tall upright and rapid-growing. Ideal to have in association with some of the winter-flowering kinds.

Calluna vulgaris. These demand a lime-free soil, rich in peat. The species flowers in late summer and autumn, although a few of the garden forms will flower outside this period, covering a period from early summer until late autumn. The annual trimming of the old flower stems is important, particularly with this species, as failure to do this results in their being leggy and lacking flowers. Correctly trimmed they will form compact plants with plenty of foliage and good flower spikes. It is recommended to trim using garden shears during the early spring, just before new growth begins.

Calluna vulgaris 'County Wicklow'. Foliage is light green becoming darker during the winter. Flowers are shell-pink from August to October. A semi-prostrate and compact plant, very suitable for the smallest of gardens.

Calluna vulgaris 'Robert Chapman'. The summer foliage is a greenish yellow with orange/red tints, and during the autumn the orange colour intensifies. A very attractive heather with flowers a soft purple in August and September. Growth upright and compact.

Calluna vulgaris 'Peter Sparkes'. Foliage is a dark grey-green with flowers deep pink. A very beautiful form with double florets also being carried on short laterals at the base of the main spikes.

Most garden centres supply heathers and there is a very wide range available, but do see that your choice suits your particular type of soil.

Hebe pinguifolia 'Pagei'. An excellent evergreen ground cover forming wide mats of rounded glaucous blue foliage, interspersed with pearly-white flower spikes in May/June. Needs plenty of light to produce maximum flowers. Height 1 foot (30 cm) spread 3 feet (90 cm).

Helianthemum. A genus closely allied to and often included with Cistus. Dwarf shrub which spreads very broadly and rapidly, and is covered for several weeks from May onwards with delicate flowers in red, pink, white or yellow. It must have full sun and will flourish even in poor dryish soils. After flowering trim it back with shears to keep it compact.

Hypericum calycinum. Known as 'Rose of Sharon' it is an extremely useful plant for clothing a bank and grows well under trees. The cup-shaped yellow flowers are 3 inches (7.5 cm) across and begin flowering in June and well into September providing it is in the sun. Needs to be trimmed in March. Height 9 inches (23 cm), spreads easily by mat-like roots.

Hypericum moserianum. This has large waxy golden flowers with crimson stamens which are freely produced in June. An improvement in many respects on the above. Height 3 feet (90 cm) with spread of 3 to 4 feet (90 cm to 1.22 m).

Lonicera pileata. A splendid ground cover that is evergreen with a low wide habit, ideal for planting in front of shrubberies and among evergreen bushes. Height 1 to 2 feet (30 to 60 cm).

Pernettya mucronata. A semi-dwarf berrying evergreen shrub with small leaves. Requires a moist and non-chalky soil in full sun. Use peat when planting and mulching. Height 2 feet to 4 feet (60 cm to 1.22 m).

Vinca. Also known as the periwinkle. This is a creeping and shade bearing plant, useful to cover bare ground, but it needs to be strictly controlled as it can be a nuisance in a small garden, becoming very invasive.

Vinca minor. Smaller and more prostrate than the above. Flowers April to September.

Vinca minor 'Bowles Variety'. Has light blue flowers from July to October. Has a tendency to grow in clumps.

Vinca minor 'Alba'. Has dark-green leaves, pointed at both ends, and white flowers in April and May.

Vinca minor 'Atropurpurea'. Has soft-purple flowers otherwise similar to the 'alba'.

Juniperus communis prostrata. This only grows 12 inches (30 cm) high but will spread 3 feet (90 cm) or more over the ground.

Juniperus sabina tamariscifolia. A most handsome type for planting, with its fresh deep green. It is also useful among other Junipers and in rockeries. Height up to 3 feet (90 cm) and spreads up to 8 feet (2.4 m).

Climbing Plants

Providing some reasonable kind of support is available then climbing plants add an extra dimension to the garden or indeed to the house.

The usual types of support include pergolas, trellises, archways, poles and house walls. Some climbing plants such as clematis cling and twine to some form of support by tendrils and others, like the honeysuckle, by twining stems. Then there are the self-clinging climbers such as ivies. Most climbers and wall plants will grow in ordinary garden soil, but all will benefit from an application of vegetable compost or leaf-mould at planting time and mulching when once established. A south- or west-facing wall of a house or garage offers a good place for planting honeysuckle and clematis providing wooden supports are fixed onto it. The clematis will need its roots in shade, particularly in a south-facing aspect. Winter-flowering jasmines grow well on a north- or east-facing wall. A climbing hydrangea, a self-clinging type, like the ivy and virginia creeper, also does well on a north or east wall.

Care needs to be taken in selecting the right plants for the right situation, because even a south-east-facing wall can be unsuitable for plants needing a southern aspect only.

Make sure any support is securely fastened onto a wall, otherwise plants will begin to flop all over the place.

A few self-clinging types include:

Hedera canariensis 'Variegata'. For a large expanse of clear wall this particular ivy is ideal. Large olive-green leaves with silver and white edging. Thrives in sun or shade but will grow on a north- or east-facing wall, but not hardy in very severe winters. Will need to be pruned to keep it in bounds.

Hedera helix 'Goldheart'. A very charming and elegant ivy with rich green foliage with a central splash of yellow. Will thrive against a north- or east-facing wall.

Hedera helix 'Jubilee'. Very pretty with small silver and green leaves. Suitable for a north- or east-facing wall. Ivies do not damage walls or buildings, though the growth should be restricted to prevent clogging up of gutterings.

Hydrangea petiolaris (Climbing Hydrangea). Deciduous and strong growing. Has rich, dark-green leaves pale-green and downy underneath, turning lemon colour in the autumn. Produces greenish-white flowers in June. Does well on a north- or east-facing wall.

Parthenocissus henryana. Deciduous and not quite hardy. Has three- and five-lobed dark-green leaves with veins which are picked out in silver and pink, and which turn red in the autumn. Does best in some shade but not on an east-facing wall.

Parthenocissus quinquefolia (Virginia Creeper). Virginia creeper grows well and shows to advantage on a south- or west-facing wall. Hardy and deciduous, with five-lobed matt-green leaves that change to orange and red in autumn. Grows well in moist soil. Needs to be summer pruned to control its denseness and spread.

Climbing Plants Needing Support
Lonicera (Honeysuckle)

These popular climbing plants prefer moist soil and are best when allowed to climb over arches or pergolas. Their roots benefit from being in the shade, and are best planted with a south- or west-facing aspect.

Lonicera japonica 'Halliana'. A splendid honeysuckle and heavily scented white-yellow flowers. Semi-evergreen, flowers from midsummer until November.

Lonicera periclymenum 'Belgica'. This is the 'Early Dutch Honeysuckle'. Has heavily scented creamy-white flowers in May and June. Deciduous.

Jasminum officinale.
This is a climber to grow near a window so that the fragrance of the white flowers can be enjoyed on fine summer evenings and in early autumn. It is

deciduous but semi-evergreen in a mild winter. It needs a south or west aspect, tied and trained for good effect. Only prune when it is necessary to thin out after flowering.

Jasminum nudiflorum (Winter-flowering Jasmine). No garden is really complete without this winter jasmine. This variety will flourish on a north- or east-facing wall. Its only failing is lack of scent, but its bright-yellow flowers add colour to a dark winter's day and into April. Prune after flowering, shortening the strongest shoots which have flowered, and cutting back others close to the old wood. Tie in the main shoots, and allow the young shoots to 'weep'.

Clematis

There are six groups available ranging from the Florida, Jackmanii and Patens to name a few. Probably the best idea would be to keep to the late-flowering varieties. Clematis grow best in rich loam containing some lime, with their roots shaded and their heads in the sun. They appreciate an annual mulch of vegetable compost on a moistened soil. When planting make sure the top of the ball of soil is 2 inches (5 cm) below the level of the soil after planting.

A south- or west-facing aspect is best for clematis although there are several which grow on a north or east wall.

Jackmanii 'Comtesse de Bouchard' (Jackmanii group). Has cyclamen pink flowers with a touch of mauve. Gracefully curved sepals. Season June to October.

Clematis 'Nelly Moser' (Patens Group). One of the best-known of this group. Has large bluish white flowers with carmine stripe. Season of flowering May, June and again in September/October (see plate 8(a)).

Climbing roses

These are in most cases sports from the bush varieties. None of them are as vigorous as a 'rambler', so they are very adaptable for training up pillars, fences and walls. There are many colours from which to choose, red, vermillion, pink, white, yellow and multi-colour shades. Newly planted climbers must be pruned to within five or six buds from the base. Prune out old wood in the autumn and tie in new growths. In March tip these to encourage laterals. There should be ample information on climbing roses at garden centres.

Vitis coignetiae

An excellent non-fruiting vine which has very large leaves that turn colour in autumn to crimson and orange shades. The plants cling by tendrils to the support provided. Very useful for rambling over outbuildings and extensive walls.

Wisteria

There are perhaps no more beautiful climbing shrubs than the wisterias, with their long drooping racemes of blue, mauve or white flowers. May and June are the usual flowering times. Planting in full sun is advised. It takes a few years for them to bloom, but they are well worth waiting for.

They need a south- or west-facing aspect.

Wisteria sinesis has racemes of mauve flowers; the flowers of 'Alba' are white.

Hard Surfacing in the Garden

A hard-surfaced area adjacent to a house – a terrace or patio – can be a very pleasant link between home and garden. It is interesting to note that the word patio, is in fact, something of a misnomer; its original meaning referred to an enclosed space open to the sky or to an inner court, a feature of many large Spanish homes. Patios, like gardens, vary a great deal. Some are open to the weather, others may be protected in whole or in part by a complete roof or what is more general a pergola-type projection from the house. Vines, creepers and climbing plants can adorn them, often providing partial shade from the glare of the sun.

As an extension to the house, the patio should be designed as such, and this means being in proportion and in relation not just to the house but to the garden as well. Consideration needs to be given as to the shape and area of a patio as well as the choice of material from which it is constructed. This is important since the material must be in harmony and link up with the material used for the house. A period cottage may call for a mellow brick or natural stone, whereas a modern brick-built dwelling may call for more complementary materials such as brick combined with paving stones.

It is wise to first sketch out your ideas on paper, and to study all the aspects bearing in mind the orientation – that is, the position of the sun at a given time, whether shade is needed, and whether the paved area will blend in with lawn, trees and shrubs which might still not be planted. A fair amount of visualization is required and it is far better to take ample time before starting the job of laying down an area destined to be a sitting out extension to the house.

Whatever type of material is decided on, an area can be vastly improved with low-growing plants such as some of the varieties of *Thymus serpyllum,* for example 'Annie Hall', with its lilac flowers. Then there is the low-growing mint *Mentha quienii,* a species that makes dense mats of dark-green aromatic foliage.

When laying paving it is a simple matter to leave a few empty squares or rectangular spaces, which can either be filled with cobbles, to provide a variation in texture, or filled with soil and planted up with culinary herbs, so handy for the kitchen. But see that any such spaces do not encroach on an area of the patio which might interfere with any chairs and tables that are likely to be set out. The area selected should be marked out accurately and excavated sufficiently to allow at least six inches (15 cm) below the finished height of the paving. Then follow with 3 inches (8 cm) of rammed hardcore, and then 1 inch (2.5 cm) of well-made concrete, and finally 1½ or 2 inches (4 cm or 5 cm) of paving. In some cases paving can be spot bedded. Actually there is ample information available in a wide range of books and magazines which cover constructing a paved area of brick or stone, or just the ordinary slabs.

However, it is a good idea when doing this work to leave a gap of at least 2 inches (5 cm) between the house wall and paving, and the finished surface of the paving will need to be 6 inches (15 cm) below the damp-proof course. The gap can be filled with pea gravel, granite chippings or shingle. Make sure there is a 1 in 40 slope away from the house. We can now consider the various types of surfacing materials.

Stone
If you are keen to have natural stone, it is worth going to some trouble to locate a supplier of quarried stone.

Quarried stone may be split and given a sawn or rubbed face for use as paving. Ascertain its durability and whether the stone surface will eventually become smooth and therefore slippery. Stone thickness will vary, depending on the size of the flags. Generally though they are between 2 and 3 inches

(50 mm and 75 mm) in thickness.

Brick paviors

The right type of brick for use in paving an area is the brick pavior. Brick paviors have been fired to be far harder than the ordinary facing brick used in house building which would soon flake and become uneven. They are more expensive but are easy to lay. The alternative is to use engineering bricks which are normally the same size as house facing bricks, but much more durable.

A more economical way to achieve a sympathetic relationship between a terrace or patio and a brick-built house is slabs and bricks together – either formally, with lines of bricks between slabs, or informally, with small areas of bricks and slabs of varying size.

Granite sets

They are grey in colour and usually cube-shaped, about half the size of a brick. Not easy to obtain except perhaps through your local council highways department that may have a quantity available as a result of digging up an old road – in order to lay tarmac surfaces. Again they could be used in conjunction with natural stone paving.

Cobbles

Cobbles are usually oval in shape, and they are not to be recommended for use in large expanses or in the making of a path, due to their being difficult to walk on. They can, however, be used to advantage to infill a small area in places within a paved area. Cobbles are often laid on end, but can be laid in random fashion with the flattish side on top over a very small area as an attractive contrast.

Pre-cast concrete slabs

With the decreasing availability of natural stone, many forms of artificial substitutes such as pre-cast concrete slabs are obtainable. For sheer convenience they are being used to pave areas to form a patio or terrace, but it is best to try and break up the monotony and regularity of a large expanse of this type of medium by separating the slabs from each other with a single row of bricks, using the broad bedding face upwards.

The important thing with pre-cast slabs is to go for a neutral shade such as a pale sand colour or the very palest of pink or very pale grey-blue.

These slabs are available in various sizes, which makes for easy laying.

For paths and areas around sculptural groups of plants, the use of shingle or washed pea gravel can be very pleasing and effective. In certain areas pea gravel and shingle will need to be contained by edging material, such as granite sets, bricks or timber, to prevent spilling over on to a border from a path.

Garden Features

A very useful and attractive feature in a garden is a pergola. It consists of a number of upright supports with overhead cross-pieces, thus forming a 'roof' over a paved area adjoining a house, or a covered walk over a pathway, or a free-standing unit in the garden.

The most popular timbers for constructing pergolas are pine or larch, which are readily available in long, straight lengths from timber merchants. However, in some cases the main supports can be in brick or stone if, for instance, this would mean that the pergola would then blend in harmoniously with the materials of the house.

Before any construction work is begun, a design should be drawn up on paper so that accurate estimates of quantities can be calculated. Try to design the pergola so that it is as simple as possible in terms of structure. The overhead cross-pieces can be shaped at one end and extend over the supports. Make sure that the design is strong by making the main timber supports at least 4 inches (10 cm) square. Also, allow for plenty of headroom, taking into consideration that any trailing or climbing plants you plan to grow will be likely to hang down. It is important to allow for a soil border so that the climbing plants are in close proximity to one or more of the supports. A selection of climbing plants suitable for pergolas is on pages 125–126.

Choosing a garden seat or bench or, indeed, any garden furniture, is to a great extent a very personal decision. Even so, the following guidelines may assist you.

In the main, the best types are constructed from cedar or teak, as both are noted for their durability, and so can be safely left outdoors. The more comfortable designs have curved backs and seats and narrow strips of wood make up the seat and back, which looks very attractive. There are some that can seat several people and these are approximately 4 to 8 feet (1.2 to 2.4 m) long.

Containers for use on a terrace or indoors are usually made from materials that range from stone, clay and wood through to fibreglass and plastic. Many manufacturers use natural materials such as elm, oak, teak and cedar to make very attractive plant tubs and other shaped containers.

The important thing to check before filling plant containers is that in each holder, small or large, you put a sufficient number of stones or pieces of broken clay pot at the bottom to allow water to pass through, but care needs to be taken to avoid external staining from the drainage holes.

As a rule, it always seems more appropriate to a garden to use natural materials whenever possible.

CHAPTER 14

BASIC TOOLS AND EQUIPMENT

Essential Tools

For anyone following the system recommended in this book and working an average-sized garden or allotment plot, a few essential tools will be needed.

1. *A lightweight hand hoe or 'scrapper'.* This has a longer blade than usual, 5 to 6 inches (13 to 15 cm) (picture 5, page 20). The scrapper is the main tool for surface cultivation of the soil and its use is described in Chapter 4.

2. *A four-pronged lightweight garden fork.* The author prefers one with wooden shaft with a T-shaped handle, as this allows for freer movement than the closed D-shaped type. A four-pronged potato fork is excellent for removing deep-rooted weeds, but rather heavy for light clearing work.

3. *A long-handled draw-hoe*, with a 6 to 8 inch (15 to 20 cm) blade, with reasonably sharp corners for use when taking out and covering flat and v-shaped drills.

4. *A light but sturdy garden rake*, with a 12 inch (30 cm) wide head with teeth 2 to 2½ inches (5 to 6.5 cm) long, and a handle of comfortable length.

5. *A planting knife*, i.e. a small builder's pointing trowel with an inch or so (2.5 cm or so) of the point cut off.

6. *A dibber* (a sharpened fork handle).

7. *Secateurs* are, of course, required when soft and hard fruits are grown.

Avoid really cheap ones and any with the blades set into solid plastic handles.

These are the most essential, but the spade does have its use, principally in the initial stage of forming the strip garden beds in the vegetable and soft fruit section in a garden, in removing soil from pathways. It is also useful for chopping up vegetable waste material for composting, as well as shovelling out mature compost from the bins.

Essential Equipment

1. Compost bins

2. Kneeling board – approximately 4 inches by 1 inch 3 feet (10 cm x 90 cm), see picture 13.

3. Wooden presser – refer to picture 13.

4. Suitable-sized weed boxes, although buckets can be used if preferred.

5. A watering can – preferably 2 gallon (9 l). A metal one would probably last longer than a plastic type.

6. Rose attachments (fine and medium) for the watering can.

7. A garden hose seems essential especially if the garden is a large one with many garden beds. Select one which is very flexible with an internal diameter of ½ inch (1.25 cm).

8. Garden lines; at least three.

9. Folding measuring rule or thin wooden strip with spacings marked on.

For very large gardens a wheelbarrow is essential. Great time-savers also for large gardens are wooden markers which define a number of rows across or along the full garden bed. One with six pegs spaced at 8 or 9 inches (20 to 23 cm). If required the pegs can be used to make 'notches' along the drawn rows, and of course, 4 or 4½ inches (10 to 11.5 cm) spacing can be achieved by 'doubling' over both in 'notching' and in marking lines. Simply draw lines between the first 8 or 9 inches (20 or 23 cm) spacing marked. Generally, wooden markers are only needed if the garden is very large and growing mainly salad and other vegetable crops. Otherwise a marking cane, a 5 foot (1.5 m) bamboo with a number of rubber bands rolled onto it and spaced as required, will prove very useful for spacing in rows already marked. In large garden plots one can also use two canes, one for marking and one for spacing in the rows.

Temporary Use Only
For the initial clearing of any plot, especially heavily weed infested, a board of 5 or 6 feet (1.5 to 1.8 m) long by 1 inch by 9 inches (2.5 by 23 cm), along with two short wooden bars, (refer to picture 1) will be needed. These are for use when clearing soil for the first time as described in Chapter 3. The use of this timber board and bars ensures the minimum amount of ground is compacted and when the board and bars are moved forward onto the already cleared area, the narrow compacted areas are then easily loosened with the fork.

ORGANIC, VEGANIC, COMPOST GROWN, INORGANIC

Information in More Specific Detail

In the Ministry of Agriculture Bulletin No. 36 'Manure and Fertilizers' (1957), there are some thirty-seven pages describing organic manures of both animal and vegetable origin. For many years commercial growers have normally used organic manures of animal origin as well as artificial fertilizers, and those small growers who do not use artificial chemical fertilizers consider themselves as 'organic growers'.

However, there are many instances when buyers of 'organically grown' produce have actually questioned just what type of organic substances are used in the growing of crops for direct human consumption, little realizing that 'organic' could be either of animal or vegetable origin or a mixture of both.

This confusion continued until the word VEGANIC – compounded from the two words VEgetable and orGANIC – was coined in 1961 by Geoffrey L. Rudd in order to make a clear distinction between organic (animal origin) and organic (vegetable origin), as the word organic continues to be used in the Ministry of Agriculture's bulletins. However, the word veganic is in Chambers Dictionary – see 'Veganic' below.

More people are now aware of the word veganic and the Ministry of Agriculture also refers to the word veganic. The Ministry of Agriculture carried out trials using veganic compost in 1975 and 1976 at Wye, Kent and the results were extremely good and conclusive. Two crops were used, carrots and lettuce.

Organic

As in the Ministry of Agriculture's Bulletin No. 36 Manures and Fertilizers (1957).

Organic Manures

Cattle dung; farmyard manure; poultry manure; dried blood; pig manure, horse dung; sewage sludge; urine; slurry; hoof and horn; meat and bone meal; feathers and feather waste; rabbit waste; rabbits' eyes and ears; guano; fishmeal; shoddy; green manures; hop manures; seaweed, etc.

Veganic

As defined in Chambers Dictionary: 'Pertaining to manuring with material which is purely vegetable organic'.

Veganic Compost

Straw; bean and pea haulms; weeds; raw fruit waste; raw vegetable trimmings; seaweed; tomato, cucumber, melon, marrow haulms; tea leaves; soft herb leaves; short grass mowings, etc.

Excluded materials although of vegetable origin include: potato peelings, haulms, rhubarb, tree leaves, sawdust, chippings, thick deep-rooted weeds, fruit tree and ornamental tree prunings, and evergreen leaves. Tree-leaf compost for applying to shrub and tree areas may include tree leaves; grass mowings; lime; soil; and straw if available.

Both types of compost – that is vegetable and the tree leaf compost – are activated by a herbal solution.

'Compost-grown'

This term, like the word organic, have caused confusion and misunderstanding, chiefly because the compost material can be of either animal or vegetable origin or both, or else be activated by some substance of animal origin, say fishmeal or urine. The word compost needs to be described more accurately such as 'animal-based compost' or 'vegetable-based compost'; the term compost-grown is too vague.

Inorganic Fertilizers

These consist of two distinct groups, artificial and natural.

Artificial fertilizers are mainly soluble compounds of the elements nigrogen, phosphorous and potassium and are produced by various factory processes.

Natural inorganic fertilizers are simply mineral substances which have been dug or otherwise extracted from the soil and finely ground. They include granite dust and rock phosphate.

APPENDIX 1

ASSEMBLING A COLD FRAME

The measurements of materials listed below are required to make up a frame unit to accommodate four Dutch lights. The actual measurements are calculated according to the average size of a butt jointed Dutch light 4 feet 11 inches by 2 feet 6½ inches (1.5 m by 762 mm) overall.

The other type of Dutch light may be the slot and tenon one, which is generally a little wider (4 feet 11 inches by 2 feet 7½ inches) (1.5 m by 813 mm) overall. The use of this size of Dutch light would mean having back-boards, top and stopper rails, and bottom front rail some 6 inches (150 mm) longer in length, in order to accommodate four Dutch lights.

Use the plan, elevations and construction detail shown in picture 27 to help you when following the Method of Construction section.

Materials Required to Make a Frame Bed Unit

Timber for the backboard Two lengths each 11 feet by 1 inch by 6 inches (38 mm by 25 mm by 150 mm).

Top rail timber One piece p.a.r. 11 feet by 1 inch by 3½ inches (3.38 m by 25 mm by 90 mm). One piece p.a.r. 11 feet by ¾ inch by 1 inch (3.38 m by 20 mm by 25 mm).

Timber posts to take backboards Four sawn stakes each approximately 2 feet by 2 inches by 3 inches (600 mm by

50 mm by 75 mm) pointed at one end of each stake.

Bottom front rail timber One sawn length 11 feet by 2 inches by 5 inches (3.38 m by 50 mm by 127 mm).

Timber for end triangles Four lengths p.a.r. 4 feet 11 inches by 1½ inches by 2 inches (1.5 m by 40 mm by 50 mm).

Eight sawn pieces Each 1 foot by ¾ inch by 3 inches (305 mm by 15 mm by 76 mm) (These are driven into the soil at each side of the bottom front rail timber to maintain correct position.)

Eight galvanized staples One each for the top end of each Dutch light and one each for driving into the stopper rail opposite staple of each Dutch light and these are then fastened with strong wire to hold each light in position, and prevent the lights from slipping down off the top flat rail.

Sufficient quantity of galvanized round wire nails For fastening backboards onto the four stakes. (These nails ought to be 2½ inches (65 mm) long.)

Quantity of galvanized round wire nails for fastening the flat top rail and stopper rails onto the top of stakes; 2 inch (50 mm) for the flat top rail, and 1½ inch (40 mm) nails to fasten the stopper rail onto the flat top rail.

Nails will also be required to fasten the triangle bars onto the top flat rail and bottom front rail. Four blocks of

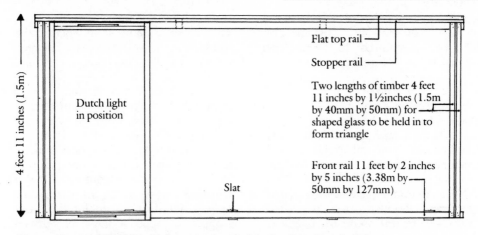

4 feet 11 inches (1.5m)

Dutch light
in position

Flat top rail

Stopper rail

Two lengths of timber 4 feet
11 inches by 1½inches (1.5m
by 40mm by 50mm) for
shaped glass to be held in to
form triangle

Front rail 11 feet by 2 inches
by 5 inches (3.38m by
50mm by 127mm)

Slat

Picture 27 (a) **Plan of cold frame unit suitable for four Dutch lights.**

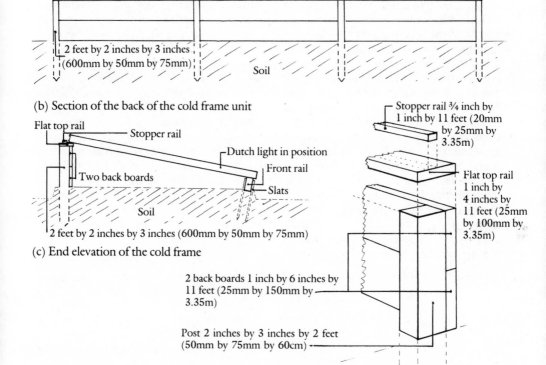

11 feet (3.38m)

2 feet by 2 inches by 3 inches
(600mm by 50mm by 75mm)

Soil

(b) Section of the back of the cold frame unit

Stopper rail ¾ inch by
1 inch by 11 feet (20mm
by 25mm by
3.35m)

Flat top rail
1 inch by
4 inches by
11 feet (25mm
by 100mm by
3.35m)

Flat top rail

Stopper rail

Two back boards

Dutch light in position

Front rail

Slats

Soil

2 feet by 2 inches by 3 inches (600mm by 50mm by 75mm)

(c) End elevation of the cold frame

2 back boards 1 inch by 6 inches by
11 feet (25mm by 150mm by
3.35m)

Post 2 inches by 3 inches by 2 feet
(50mm by 75mm by 60cm)

(d) Construction detail of the back corner of the cold frame wood – each 8 inches by 4 inches by 2 inches (200 mm by 100 mm by 50 mm) – required for ventilation purposes (see picture 21).

Method of Construction
Two strong lines are stretched tightly along what is to be the back of the frame bed to take four Dutch lights. One line just above soil level and one at a height of 12 inches (30 cm) from the ground.

Next drive in a stake at each end of the correct distance – that is 11 feet (3 m) – to be just above the height of the top taut string line.

Then measure out 3 feet 8 inches (1.2 m) from each end stake, and drive in the two remaining stakes, again to finish (temporarily) just above the height of the top string line. Check the tautness of the top string line – the one 12 inches (30 cm) above the ground level – then tap the four stakes to the height of the top string line. The backboards are then nailed onto the stakes using the 2½ inch (65 mm) nails onto the inner side (with the stakes showing only on the outside of the frame bed) – at the back, as it were.

Then fasten the flat top rail onto the tops of the four stakes, leaving the inside of the top rail flush with the inside of the backboards. Next, fasten the stopper rail onto the flat top rail. To get the correct position of the bottom front rail use a Dutch light. The front rail 11 feet (3.38 m) long when in the right position, is held in place between the wooden slats driven into the ground so that the front bottom rail rests between them. When checking with a Dutch light, allow for a projection beyond the bottom front rail by an inch (25 mm). This is so that, when the lights are fixed into position, rain is allowed to run off into the pathway clear of the bottom front rail. It also makes for easy lifting of the lights. Staples are then driven into the top stopper rail opposite the staples driven into the top rail of the Dutch light – that is the centre of each light. The wooden bars are then fixed at the very end of the frame unit and shaped pieces of glass slipped in between the two bars. Allow about ½ inch (12 mm) between the two bars for the glass pieces to slide in easily.

The frame bed is then ready for cultivations without the Dutch lights. The lights are placed in position between the staples on the light and staples on the stopper rail and strong wire fastens the two staples together. (One wire is tied to each Dutch light.) The lights should be placed close to each other but not in the slightest degree wedged. If correctly positioned the lower end of each light will be in a straight level row.

APPENDIX 2

DIMENSIONS OF A
TWIN COMPOST BIN

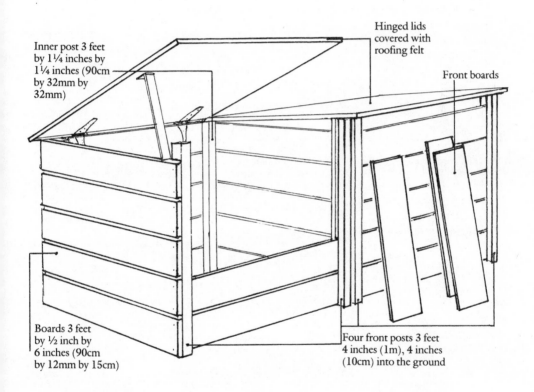

Inner post 3 feet by 1¼ inches by 1¼ inches (90cm by 32mm by 32mm)

Hinged lids covered with roofing felt

Front boards

Boards 3 feet by ½ inch by 6 inches (90cm by 12mm by 15cm)

Four front posts 3 feet 4 inches (1m), 4 inches (10cm) into the ground

Timber requirements for twin compost bin:
5 lengths 6 feet by ½ inch by 6 inches (1.83m by 12mm by 15cm)
15 lengths 3 feet by ½ inch by 6 inches (90cm by 12mm by 15cm)
7 posts 3 feet 4 inches by 2 inches by 2 inches (1m by 5cm by 5cm)
4 inner posts 3 feet by 1¼ inches by 1¼ inches (90cm by 32mm by 32mm)
10 front boards 3 feet (90cm), p.a.r.
2 lids 3 feet 4 inches by 3 feet 2 inches (1m by 95cm)

SUPPLIERS

Manufacturer and supplier of compost containers, tools (including the scrapper), Herbal Compost Maker and Dutch lights).

> Veganic Garden Products,
> Gatehouse Cottage,
> Heath Farm Road,
> Worstead,
> Norfolk NR28 9AH.

Supplier of Maxicrop natural seaweed plant food.

> Maxicrop Ltd.,
> 21 London Road, Great Shelford,
> Cambridge CB2 5DF.

Manufacturers of Dutch light greenhouses and Dutch lights.

> F. Pratten & Co. Ltd.,
> Charlton Road,
> Midsomer Norton,
> Bath,
> Avon BA3 4AG.

> Messrs. Robinsons of Winchester,
> Robinson House,
> Winnall Industrial Estate,
> Winchester SO23 8CH.

USEFUL ADDRESSES

The Royal Horticultural Society,
Vincent Square,
London SW1P 2PE

The Herb Society,
77 Great Peter Street,
London SW1P 2EZ.

The National Allotments and Leisure
Gardens Society Ltd.,
22 High Street,
Flitwick,
Bedford MK45 1DT.

INDEX

Activator, herbal, 16, 23, 25–30
Aeration of soil, 13, 21
Animal organics, 10–11, 17
   dangers of, 10, 11
   definition of, 132
   dung, 10, 52
   manures, 9
   wastes, 9–10
Apples, 79–83
   cooking, 82–83
   dessert, 81–82
Aubergine (eggplant), 99–100

Bacteria, 10–11, 16, 25, 27
Beans:
   broad, 45–46
   climbing French, 48–49
   dwarf French, 48
   runner, 49–50
Beetroot, 42
Blackcurrants, 72–73
Boards, 130–131
   to kneel on, 23
   to work from, 15
Brassicas, 51–56
   roots and stems of, 27–28
Brick paviors, 128
Broccoli, 55–56
Bruce, Maye, *From Vegetable Waste to Fertile Soil*, 9
Brussels sprouts, 54

Cabbage, 53–54
Capsicum (sweet pepper), 98–99
Carrots:
   in outdoor garden beds, 40–41
   in cold frame, 89

Cauliflower, 54–55
Chalk and limestone soils, 13–14
Chamomile lawn, 105
Chemical fertilizers (artificial), 10
Clay soils, 14, 23
Climbing plants, 124–126
Cloches, 85–86
   ventilation of, 86
Cobbles, 128
Cold frame (Dutch lights), 86–87
   assembly of, 134–136
   ventilation of, 87–91, 134, 136
Compost:
   bins/containers, 23–24, 137
   fine, 24–27
   making, 24–28
   rough, 27–28
   straw box, 28
   suitable materials, 24–26
   tree-leaf, 29–30
   unsuitable materials, 27
   water, 29
Cucumbers:
   in cold frame, 89–91
   in unheated greenhouse, 96–97
   outdoor ridge, 43–44
Cultivation, 20
   surface, 7, 9, 12, 17, 18, 21, 101–102
   without digging, 20

Dutch lights, 85–87
   for cold frame, 134–136
   for cold frame cropping, 87–92

Earthworms, 10–11, 13–14, 25
Equipment, essential, 130–131

From Vegetable Waste to Fertile Soil (Maye, Bruce), 9
Fruit, Growing, 70–84
   apple and pear, 79–84
   soft fruits, 70–78

Glossary, 132–133
Garden design, 101–104
Garden features, 128–129
Gooseberries, 76–78
Granite dust, 70, 133
Grass mowings, 23–25, 27–29
Granite sets, 128
Grass water, 29
Greenhouse, Unheated, 92–94
   ventilation of, 93, 95, 97–98
Ground cover plants, 121–124

Hard surfacing, 120–128
   brick paviors, 128
   cobbles, 128
   granite sets, 128
   pre-cast concrete slabs, 128
   stone, 127–128
Heathers, 121–124
Hedging, 111–113
Herbal activator, 16, 23–30
   supplier, 138
Herbs, 61–69
   annual, 61, 65–66
   biennial, 61–2
   perennial, 62–69

Humus, 12–14, 23, 70, 101

Intensive Gardening, (Rosa Dalziel O'Brien), 9

Kale (curly), 56

Lawns:
  chamomile, 105
  clearing area for a lawn, 105
  using seed, 106
  using turf, 105-106
Leeks, 50–51
Lettuce:
  in cold frame, 87–88
  in outdoor garden beds, 37–39
  in unheated greenhouse, 94–95
  seed sowing and planting, 37–39
Lime, 16, 28, 133
Loam soils, 13

Manures (green), 24, 28–29, 132
  for composting, 28–29
Melons:
  in cold frame, 91–92
  in unheated greenhouse, 97–98

Non-compaction, 9, 11, 14
  advantages of, 11, 14
No-digging (surface cultivation), 11–12, 20, 58, 101–102
  benefits from, 9, 11, 18, 70, 101–102
Nuts, 110

O'Brien, Rosa Dalziel, *Intensive Gardening,* 9
Onions:
  from sets, 47
  salad, 41–42
Organic:
  animal dung, 10, 52
  animal manures, 9, 132
  animal wastes, 9–10
  definition of, 132
  diseases of, 9, 11

Paths:
  in the leisure garden, 128
  in the vegetable garden, 11, 18–20
Patio:
  construction of, 127
  materials to use, 127–128
Peas, 46–47
Pears, 83–84
Peat, 59, 86, 113, 119, 122
Potatoes, in garden beds, 58–60
Pre-cast concrete slabs, 128

Radishes:
  in outdoor garden beds, 39–40
  in cold frame, 88–89
Raised garden beds, 18–20
  advantages of, 11, 18–20, 35
  in unheated greenhouse, 93–94
  making, 19–20
Raspberries, 74–76
Red and white currants, 73–74

Salad crops:
  in outdoor garden beds, 37–44
  in cold frame, 86–91
  in unheated greenhouse, 92–96
Sandy soils, 13
Scrapper, 15
  description of, 20–21
  use of, 20–22
Seaweed, 132
  liquid feeds, 29, 38–48, 50–53, 55–57
  Maxicrop, 29
Seed sowing and planting methods of, 30–32
Shallots, 47
Shrubs, 113–121
Silver sand, 30
Soft fruits, 70–78
Soil:
  aeration, 13, 21
  bacteria, 10–11, 16, 25, 27
  chalk and limestone, 13–14
  clay, 14

conversion of, 33
loam, 13
non-compaction of, 9, 11, 14
sandy, 13
transformation of, 21
Soot, 20, 29, 30, 46
Soot water, 29
Stone, 127–128
Straw:
  compost box, 28
  new into old, 29
  for compost, 25
  for paths, 19–20
  use in clearing land, 16
Strawberries, 70–72
Swedes, 58
Sweet corn, 56–58

Tares, 28–29
Tomatoes:
  in outdoor garden beds, 42–43
  in unheated greenhouse, 95–96
Tools, essential, 130, (*see also* equipment)
Trees for the garden, 106–111
Tree-leaf compost, 29–30

Vegetables, 45–60
Veganic:
  compost making, 24–26
  definition of, 132

Watering, 35–36
  cold frame, 88–92
  methods of, 35, 36
  strawed areas, 16
  unheated greenhouse, 93–99
Weeds, 9, 11, 12, 33
  annual, 15, 17, 23–24, 33
  clearing, 15–17, 19, 21–22, 105
  deep-rooted perennial, 15–16, 27–28, 33, 105
  for composting, 15, 21, 23, 24, 28, 34
  value of, 33–34
Weeding, 33–34, 38
  two part, 33–34